FINANCIAL REGULATORS

FINANCIAL REGULATORS

UNITED STATES GOVERNMENT
ACCOUNTABILITY OFFICE

Novinka Books
New York

For permission to use material from this book please contact us:
Telephone 631-231-7269; Fax 631-231-8175
Web Site: http://www.novapublishers.com

Library of Congress Cataloging-in-Publication Data

Available Upon Request

ISBN 978-1-60692-042-8

Published by Nova Science Publishers, Inc. ✣ New York

CONTENTS

ABBREVIATIONS

CFTC	Commodity Futures Trading Commission
CPDF	Central Personnel Data File
EEO	Equal Employment Opportunity
FCA	Farm Credit Administration
FDIC	Federal Deposit Insurance Corporation
FHFB	Federal Housing Finance Board
FIRREA	Financial Institutions Reform, Recovery and Enforcement Act
IT	information technology
NCUA	National Credit Union Administration
OCC	Office of the Comptroller of the Currency
OFHEO	Office of Federal Housing Enterprise Oversight
OPM	Office of Personnel Management
OTS	Office of Thrift Supervision
SEC	Securities and Exchange Commission
SSP	Senior Staff Position

CORRESPONDENCE

June 18, 2007

Congressional Requesters:

The federal government must adapt to a range of major trends and challenges in the nation and the world, and to respond, it must have the institutional capacity to plan more strategically, identify and react more expeditiously, and focus on achieving results. Critical to the success of this transformation are the federal government's people—its human capital. Yet the government has not transformed, in many cases, how it classifies, compensates, develops, and motivates its employees to achieve maximum results within available resources and existing authorities. One of the questions being addressed as the federal government transforms is how to update its compensation system to be more market based and performance oriented.[1] In this type of system, organizations consider the skills, knowledge, and performance of employees as well as the labor market when making pay decisions.

Congress has recognized the need for flexibility in how selected agencies compensate employees. Congress granted the federal financial regulatory agencies the flexibility to establish their own compensation systems recognizing that the existing approach to compensating employees could impede these agencies' ability to recruit and retain employees critical to meeting their organizational missions. In addition to the flexibility provided to the agencies over the years, Congress also directed most of the agencies to seek to maintain pay comparability and to consult with each other in doing so to ensure the agencies do not compete with each other for employees.[2] The 10 federal financial regulatory agencies reviewed in this report are the Commodity Futures Trading Commission (CFTC), the Farm Credit Administration (FCA), the Federal Deposit Insurance Corporation (FDIC), the Federal Housing Finance Board (FHFB), the Board of Governors of the Federal Reserve System (Federal Reserve Board), the National Credit Union Administration (NCUA), the Office of the

Comptroller of the Currency (OCC), the Office of Federal Housing Enterprise Oversight (OFHEO), the Office of Thrift Supervision (OTS), and the Securities and Exchange Commission (SEC).

In our prior work, we identified key practices for effective performance management systems that collectively create a "line of sight" showing how team, unit, and individual performance can contribute to overall organizational goals and help individuals understand the connection between their daily activities and the organization's success.[3]

In your February 2006 letter, you noted that the financial regulatory agencies are at different stages of implementing their performance-based pay systems and compensation authorities and that an examination of how they are implementing their systems could be valuable to other agencies pursuing performance-based pay systems. Our past work looking at agencies' implementation of performance management and performance-based pay systems has shown that better linking pay to performance is very much a work in progress at the federal level.[4]

In response to your request, this report examines (1) how the performance-based pay systems of 10 federal financial regulatory agencies are aligned with six key practices for effective performance management systems, (2) the actions 10 federal regulatory agencies have taken to assess and implement comparability in pay and benefits with each other, and (3) the extent to which employees in selected occupations have moved between or left any of the agencies.

For purposes of this review, we focused on six key practices for effective performance management, which are more closely related to planning, rating, and rewarding individual performance:[5]

1. Align individual performance expectations with organizational goals.
2. Connect performance expectations to crosscutting goals.
3. Use competencies to provide a fuller assessment of performance.
4. Link pay to individual and organizational performance.
5. Make meaningful distinctions in performance.
6. Involve employees and stakeholders to gain ownership of performance management systems.

In this report, we present important aspects of the agencies' implementation of the practices of linking pay to individual and organizational performance, which includes providing adequate safeguards to help ensure fairness and guard against abuse, and making meaningful distinctions in performance. We discuss the agencies' implementation of the four other practices included in the list in appendix III.

To address our first objective, we analyzed the selected agencies' performance management and pay systems' guidance, policies, and procedures and other related documents; interviewed key agency officials and representatives of unions or other employee groups; examined a small, select set of employees' individual performance plans to illustrate annual performance expectations for employees; and analyzed agencies' performance management data, such as the distribution of performance ratings and performance-based pay increases. The individual performance plans, selected in conjunction with agency officials to reflect a mix of key locations, occupations, and grade levels at each agency, as well as the performance management data from each agency that we examined, pertained to each agency's last completed performance appraisal cycle when we began this review.[6]

To address our second objective, we analyzed relevant statutes and legislative histories for the selected agencies; reviewed the most recent pay and benefits surveys from these agencies; obtained agency pay and benefits data; and discussed agencies' informal interactions to assess pay comparability with agency officials. For the third objective, we analyzed data from the Central Personnel Data File (CPDF), which includes information on pay, benefits, personnel actions, and other data to support statistical analyses of executive branch personnel management programs, to determine employee movement.

We conducted various inspections and electronic testing of agency data obtained for the first objective for reasonableness and the presence of any obvious or potential errors in accuracy and completeness. We also reviewed related agency documentation, interviewed agency officials knowledgeable about the data, and brought to the attention of these officials any concerns or discrepancies we found with the data for correction or updating. On the basis of these procedures, we believe the data are sufficiently reliable for use in the analyses presented in this report. Our data collection strategies were not designed to guarantee that we would identify all potential examples of how agencies may have implemented the various practices. An agency may have implemented a particular practice even if it is not specifically mentioned in the report. We did not independently verify the data in the pay and benefits comparability surveys the consultants conducted for the agencies or the pay and benefits data we received from the agencies. On the basis of our data reliability testing of CPDF data, we believe the CPDF data are sufficiently reliable for this review. Appendix I provides additional information on our scope and methodology. We conducted our work from February 2006 through June 2007 in accordance with generally accepted government auditing standards.

RESULTS IN BRIEF[*]

Overall, the federal financial regulators have implemented key practices for effective performance management systems in ways that consider the unique needs of their organizational cultures and structures, but some have opportunities to improve implementation of certain practices as they continue to refine their systems. All of the regulators awarded some pay increases during the appraisal cycles we reviewed that were linked to employees' performance ratings. However, CFTC and SEC also provided across-the-board increases to employees, even to the few employees who had not received acceptable performance ratings, weakening the linkage of pay to performance. Officials from both agencies stated that in the future, annual pay adjustments will not be awarded to unsuccessful performers. While all of the regulators built safeguards into their performance management systems to enhance credibility and fairness, SEC did not establish and communicate performance standards to its non-executives, which could compromise the credibility of the system. Several regulators did not fully implement the safeguard of providing overall ratings and pay increase results to all employees, affecting employees' ability to understand where they stood in their organizations. As a result, some regulators have opportunities to strengthen an important safeguard for providing transparency within their performance-based pay systems.

The financial regulators have hired external compensation consultants to conduct individual, formal comparability surveys, exchanged pay and benefits information, explored the feasibility of conducting a common survey, or adjusted pay and benefits to seek to maintain comparability requirements. Although officials said that they have adjusted pay and benefits partly based on the results of their comparability efforts, there is some variation in pay ranges and benefit packages among the agencies. For example, the regulators have varying minimum and maximum pay ranges for similar job series and offer different benefits such as tuition reimbursement and supplemental

---

[*] This book is an excerpted indexed version of GAO Report GAO-07-678, Dated June 2007

retirement plans. When discussing the reasons that may contribute to this variation, agency officials said that the year the agencies first became subject to comparability provisions, budget constraints, and the needs and preferences of the workforce play a role in compensation decisions and contribute to this variation. Furthermore, officials emphasized that it was not their goal to have identical pay and benefits packages; rather, they considered pay and benefits as a total package when seeking to maintain pay and benefits comparability and when setting pay policies aimed at recruiting and retaining employees.

From fiscal years 1990 through 2006, the movement of employees among the financial regulators was very low and presented no discernible trend over the period, but 86 percent (13,433) of the 15,627 employees leaving the regulators voluntarily (i.e., moving or resigning), resigned from the federal government.[7] The number of employees who moved to another financial regulator ranged from a low of 16 of 1,362 who moved or resigned in fiscal year 1997 to a high of 97 of 1,229 who moved or resigned in fiscal year 1991. The total number of financial regulator employees was 15,400 (1997) and 19,796 (1991) during those 2 years. (Federal Reserve Board data are excluded from the federal government's personnel database and are not included in these analyses.) Some agency officials told us that they believe that the Financial Institutions Reform, Recovery and Enforcement Act (FIRREA) comparability provision and similar provisions in subsequent laws applicable to financial regulators have been effective in ensuring that regulators' pay and benefits are generally comparable among the 10 agencies, which probably helps minimize employee movement among financial regulatory agencies. The movement of mission-critical employees, including accountants, attorneys, auditors, examiners, economists, financial analysts, investigators, information technology specialists, and business specialists, to a different financial regulator also produced no discernible trends.

This report includes recommendations to CFTC, FCA FHFB, NCUA, OFHEO, and SEC. FCA, FHFB, and OFHEO should communicate the overall results of the performance appraisal and pay increase decisions to all employees agencywide while protecting individual confidentiality. NCUA, CFTC, and SEC should work with unions to communicate the overall results of the performance appraisal and pay increase decisions to all employees agencywide while protecting individual confidentiality. SEC should clearly communicate the criteria for making performance rating and pay increase decisions to non-executive employees and should assess senior executives' performance at the end of the performance appraisal cycle regardless of the amount of funding available for performance-based pay increases.

We provided a copy of the draft report to the Chairman, Commodity Futures Trading Commission; Chairman of the Board and Chief Executive Officer, Farm Credit Administration; Chairman, Federal Deposit Insurance Corporation; Chairman, Federal Housing Finance Board; Chairman, Board of Governors of the Federal Reserve System; Chairman, National Credit Union Administration; Comptroller of the

Currency, Office of the Comptroller of the Currency; Director, Office of Federal Housing Enterprise Oversight; Director, Office of Thrift Supervision; and Chairman, Securities and Exchange Commission, for review and comment. We received written comments from six of the agencies. They generally agreed with the findings and recommendations. See appendixes VI, VII, VIII, IX, X, and XI for letters received from CFTC, the Federal Reserve Board, FHFB, NCUA, OFHEO, and SEC. These six agencies, along with the other four, also provided clarifying and technical comments, which we have incorporated as appropriate. Several agencies described actions they plan to take to address the recommendation to communicate the overall results of the performance appraisal and pay increase decisions to all employees on an agency-wide basis while protecting individual confidentiality.

Background

The 10 federal financial regulatory agencies in our review vary in size, mission, funding structure, whether they bargain with a union, and how long they have been implementing aspects of performance-based pay systems. For example, FHFB is the smallest agency with just over 120 employees, while FDIC, the largest agency, had more than 4,300 employees as of September 2006 and has been implementing pay for performance since 1998. Likewise, these agencies regulate a range of activities including banking and securities and futures. Appendix II includes the financial regulators' missions, funding structures, and whether they are unionized and bargain with a union over pay and benefits.

Under Title 5 of the U.S. Code, the financial regulatory agencies have the flexibility to establish their own compensation programs without regard to various statutory provisions on classification and pay for executive branch agencies. At the same time these financial regulators received increased flexibility regarding compensation, Congress also generally required that they seek compensation comparability with each other. A provision in FIRREA requires six agencies—FDIC, OCC, NCUA, FHFB, FCA, and OTS—in establishing and adjusting compensation and benefits, to inform each other and Congress of such compensation and benefits, and to seek to maintain comparability regarding compensation and benefits.[8] Additional FIRREA provisions require FCA, FHFB, NCUA, OCC, and OTS to seek to maintain compensation and benefit comparability with the Federal Reserve Board.[9] Although the Federal Reserve Board is under no obligation to seek to maintain compensation or benefit comparability with these or any of the other financial regulators, it has agreed to share compensation information with the other financial regulators.

Table 1. Federal Financial Regulator Pay Comparability Legislative Provisions

			Comparability Agencies									
			FIRREA Agencies							Federal Reserve Board		
Agency	Comparability Provisions	Year of provision	FCA	FDIC	FHFB	NCUA	OCC	OTS	CFTC		OFHEO	SEC
CFTC	Post-FIRREA	2002	x	x	x	x	x	x				
FCA	FIRREA	1989		x	x	x	x	x		x		
FDIC	FIRREA	1989	x		x	x	x	x				
FHFB	FIRREA	1989	x	x		x	x	x		x		
NCUA	FIRREA	1989	x	x	x		x	x		x		
OCC	FIRREA	1989	x	x	x	x		x		x		
OFHEO	Post-FIRREA	1992		x			x	x		x		
OTS	FIRREA	1989	x	x	x	x	x			x		
SEC	Post-FIRREA	2002	x	x	x	x	x	x	x			
FRB	Not required but shares information with a number of agencies regarding compensation and benefits											

Source: GAO analysis of comparability legislative provisions.

The other three agencies are subject to their own compensation comparability provisions. As required by its 1992 enabling legislation, OFHEO must maintain comparability with the compensation of employees from the Federal Reserve Board, OCC, FDIC, and OTS and consult with those agencies in that regard.[10] In 2002 legislation, SEC and CFTC were placed under comparability requirements. SEC must consult with and seek to maintain compensation comparability with FDIC, OCC, NCUA, FHFB, FCA, OTS and CFTC.[11] However, as shown in table 1, this legislation did not require these agencies to seek to maintain compensation comparability with SEC. Similarly, CFTC must consult and seek to maintain compensation comparability with the six FIRREA agencies, but those agencies are not required to seek to maintain compensation comparability with CFTC.[12]

We previously identified key practices for effective performance management based on public sector organizations' experiences both here and abroad.[13] High-performing organizations seek to create pay, incentive, and reward systems that clearly link employee knowledge, skills, and contributions to organizational results. Performance-based systems reward employees according to their performance by using performance ratings as the basis for pay increases. Linking pay to performance can help to create a performance-oriented culture by providing monetary incentives to become a top- performing employee. At the same time, as a precondition to linking pay to performance, performance management systems need to provide adequate safeguards to ensure fairness and guard against abuse. Providing adequate safeguards that help to ensure transparency can improve the credibility of the performance-based pay system by promoting fairness and trust. Safeguards can include establishing clear criteria for making rating decisions and determining merit increases, and providing overall results of performance rating and pay increase decisions to all employees, while protecting confidentiality. Effective performance management systems also make meaningful distinctions between acceptable and outstanding performance of individuals and appropriately reward those who perform at the highest level. As we have previously reported, effective performance management systems can provide management with the objective and fact-based information it needs to reward top performance and provide the necessary information and documentation to deal with poor performers.[14]

Financial Regulators Generally Have Linked Pay to Performance and Made Distinctions in Performance, but Opportunities Exist for Improvements

Overall, the federal financial regulators have implemented key practices for effective performance management systems in ways that consider the unique needs of their organizational cultures and structures, but some have not fully implemented certain practices. For purposes of this section, we focus on the regulators' implementation of the two key practices of (1) linking pay to performance (which includes building in safeguards), and (2) making meaningful distinctions in performance. First, we found that while the regulators generally linked pay to performance, two regulators awarded across-the-board increases to employees regardless of their performance. Second, while most regulators generally used safeguards in varying ways to increase transparency, one did not establish and communicate performance standards to its non-executives, which resulted in questions about how decisions were made and could compromise the credibility of the performance system. Third, many regulators did not fully implement the safeguard of providing overall ratings and pay results to all employees, which reduced the transparency of their performance-based pay systems. Fourth, we found that while most regulators used multiple rating levels to make meaningful distinctions in performance, employees were usually concentrated in one or two rating categories and all had very few poor performers. Finally, one agency did not complete performance ratings for senior officers due to lack of funding for pay increases, thereby missing an opportunity to provide valuable feedback. For information about the other four key practices as well as additional material pertaining to the linking pay to performance practice, see appendix III.[15]

Financial Regulators Generally Have Linked Pay to Performance, but Two Regulators Still Provided Increases to Performers at All Levels

All of the regulators awarded some performance-based increases during the appraisal cycles we reviewed that were linked to employees' performance ratings, although two financial regulators also provided annual pay adjustments to employees, regardless of performance, during the appraisal cycles we reviewed. Specifically, CFTC provided an across-the-board pay increase to all employees to be equivalent to the cost of living adjustment received by General Schedule employees of the federal government in January 2006. During the 2005 appraisal cycle, SEC also provided all employees an across-the-board pay adjustment of 2.1 percent, regardless of their performance.[16] SEC officials noted that this across-the-board pay adjustment was in accordance with the negotiated compensation agreement with the union.[17] While the percentages of employees rated as unsuccessful or unacceptable at CFTC and SEC during those cycles were extremely small (less than 1 percent), these agencies lost opportunities to reinforce the linkage of pay to performance in their performance management systems. CFTC officials told us that the performance-based pay portion of the new performance management system that will begin on July 1, 2007, will require a minimum threshold performance rating for an employee to be eligible for a pay increase.[18] SEC and its union are currently negotiating implementation of a new Compensation and Benefits Agreement, which provides that employees rated as unacceptable will not receive annual pay adjustments. SEC officials acknowledged that a negative perception occurs when employees who are not performing satisfactorily receive a pay increase.

Most of the financial regulators used their rating systems to differentiate individual performance to award performance-based increases and reward top performers during the appraisal cycles we reviewed. Furthermore, all of the agencies also provided increases that, while not directly linked to performance ratings, considered employee performance in some way. These increases included special bonuses or awards given to individuals or teams for special accomplishments or contributions, as well as promotions and within-pay-band increases. For example, FCA provided Achievement or Special Act Awards to employees for significant achievements or innovations towards a special program, project, or assignment that contributed to the agency's or organizational unit's mission, goals, and objectives. To receive these awards, employees had to have performed their regular duties at least at a fully successful level of performance. FCA also provided some pay increases for competitive and noncompetitive promotions during the completed appraisal cycle we reviewed.

Pay increases linked to performance ratings accounted for only part of the total increases awarded to individual employees during the appraisal cycles we reviewed. See appendix III for more information on the different ways in which the regulators translated performance ratings into pay increases and budgeted for performance-based increases, as well as more information on other pay increases that involved considerations of performance.

Financial Regulators Generally Used Safeguards to Increase Transparency, but SEC Did Not Establish or Communicate Performance Standards for Its Non-executive Employees

All of the financial regulatory agencies have built safeguards into their performance management systems to enhance the credibility and fairness of their systems, although they varied in how safeguards have been implemented. For example, with the exception of SEC, the agencies have used the safeguard of establishing and communicating (1) standards for differentiating among performance rating categories and (2) criteria for performance-based pay decisions, thus enhancing transparency, which can improve employee confidence in the performance management system. (See app. III for information on the financial regulators' implementation of additional safeguards.)

CFTC's four-level rating system (i.e., unsuccessful, successful, highly successful, and exemplary) defined the successful level of performance for areas that CFTC had identified as critical to employees' job performance, and included some information on how to distinguish variations from the successful level of performance. However, an employee representative at CFTC maintained that the rating level descriptions did not sufficiently communicate to employees the skills and behaviors employees needed to demonstrate in order to move, for example, from the "successful" to the "highly successful" level. Employee representatives stated that even though there was helpful guidance on distinguishing between levels of performance in a CFTC manual, these descriptions were hard to understand and most employees did not refer to the CFTC manual for guidance. An agency official told us that the revised performance management system that went into effect in October 2006 is a five-level system, and includes descriptions of all five performance levels rather than only the successful rating level described in the system it replaced.

Similarly, OFHEO defined how employees would be rated on its five-level rating scale for each of the performance elements included in their performance plans. These performance standards defined the middle level of performance (fully successful), and included what the rater should look at to determine if an employee is performing better or worse than this benchmark. An employee's performance for each element was assessed and a total score was determined. OFHEO further distinguished between "high" and "low" levels within rating categories. For example, a rating of "outstanding" would be classified as being in either the high or low level of the outstanding rating category based on the performance score the employee received. Merit increases at OFHEO have been determined directly by employees' performance ratings, so employees could ascertain the merit increases they would receive for given performance ratings. For example, an employee rated "high" commendable receives a higher merit pay increase than one who is rated "low" commendable. OFHEO employee working group members noted that both supervisors and employees understand how the performance elements and standards have been applied through rating decisions, and they stated that employees generally understood what was expected of them to attain higher levels of performance and associated merit increases. However, an employee working group member also commented that when distinguishing between performance rating levels, some managers seemed to apply the performance standards more effectively than others, which could result in differences in how rating decisions were made.

At FDIC, for non-executive/non-manager employees to be eligible for performance-based pay increases, employees had to first earn a "meets expectations" rating. Then, in a second process called the "Pay for Performance" system, FDIC non-executive/non-managers were placed into one of four pay groups, based on an assessment of total performance and corporate contributions as compared with other employees in the same pay pool.[19] The pay for performance program was essentially comparative, meaning that the contributions and performance of each employee were evaluated and rewarded on a relative basis within his or her pay pool, as compared to peers. According to union representatives, employees were not informed about how management made the distinctions in pay increase groupings. According to FDIC officials, there are no definitive descriptions or definitions of the performance levels for each of the three pay groups because employees are assessed compared to each other, not against fixed standards. Officials also said that information on the system for determining pay groups was provided to all employees in early 2006 after the compensation and benefits agreement became effective, when the system was first rolled out, and is explained to new employees at orientation. We did not determine how widespread the concern about how management made distinctions in pay increase groupings was among FDIC employees.

In contrast, SEC officials did not establish standards upon which to base rating decisions for non-executive employees, nor did they communicate criteria used to make performance-based pay decisions to these employees. For its non-executive employees, SEC used a two-level rating system in which individuals' performance was rated as acceptable or unacceptable. According to agency management, SEC followed the definitions under Title 5 that are used by the rest of the government for differentiating between acceptable and unacceptable performance.[20] However, SEC did not establish written performance standards for appraising employees' performance as acceptable or unacceptable.

To determine performance-based pay increase amounts for non-executive employees, SEC developed a second phase process that involved making distinctions in contributions for those individuals who received a summary performance rating of acceptable. As part of the second phase, employees and their supervisors submitted contribution statements summarizing the employees' accomplishments during the appraisal cycle. Using the summary statements and the supervisors' own assessments, supervisors placed employees into one of four categories: (1) made contributions of the highest quality, (2) made contributions of high quality, (3) made contributions of quality, and (4) made no significant contribution beyond an acceptable level of performance. Next, a compensation committee within each office or division evaluated the contribution statements and the supervisors' placements. For each employee, the committee recommended a merit pay increase ranging from zero to 4.41 percent (corresponding to "steps" 0 to 3) to an official from each office or division, who made the final determination of the employee's merit increase.[21]

However, SEC did not develop criteria to differentiate between the four contribution categories that the compensation committees considered when recommending merit pay step increase amounts. In addition, SEC employee representatives told us that it was not clear to employees how the contribution statements and the subsequent supervisory recommendations were translated into the decisions about the four contribution categories into which employees would be placed. SEC officials noted that employees received copies of narratives written by their supervisors to describe the employees' contributions; however, they acknowledged that the system could be more transparent. According to SEC officials, in an effort to increase transparency in the future, they plan to share with employees information on supervisors' preliminary recommendations on ratings that are provided to the compensation committee, so that employees can see into which of the four contribution categories they were recommended for placement and the supporting documentation. If the committee changes an initial recommendation from a supervisor, SEC will provide the employee with the rationale for the change. An agency official indicated they are developing broad statements, such as "the committee had a broader perspective of employee contributions," that address a range of possible reasons for changes.

Some Financial Regulators Did Not Fully Implement the Safeguard of Providing Overall Ratings and Pay Increase Results to All Employees, Which Would Increase Transparency in Their Performance-Based Pay Systems

The extent to which the financial regulators shared the overall results of performance ratings and pay increase decisions with all employees varied, and some agencies did not make this information widely available to employees. We have previously reported that the safeguard of communicating the overall results of performance appraisal and pay increase decisions while protecting individual confidentiality can improve transparency by letting employees know where they stand in the organization.[22] An employee's summary performance rating conveys information about how well an employee has performed against established performance standards, which is important, but not sufficient to provide a clear picture of how the employee's performance compares with that of other employees within the organization. When the organization communicates where an employee stands, management can gain credibility by having honestly disclosed to the employee the basis for making pay, promotion, or developmental opportunity decisions that may have been based upon relative performance.

The Federal Reserve Board communicated the overall results of the performance appraisal decisions to all employees by sharing annual performance rating distributions with all employees, disaggregated by division. Since this system for determining the amounts of performance-based increases for individuals based on their performance ratings is essentially driven by formula, employees know what their merit increases will be relative to others after receiving their performance ratings.

At FDIC, the distribution of pay group assignments for all non-executive/ non-manager employees who passed the first assessment process is fixed by the negotiated agreement with the union, so those employees know how performance-based pay increases will be distributed and the amounts of increases received by the various pay groups. Further, FDIC officials told us that, in accordance with the collective bargaining agreement, after completion of each annual pay for performance cycle they share data on the results of the pay grouping decisions for employees covered by the bargaining unit contract with union representatives. These include summary pay group data analyzed according to the agreement with the union, such as certain demographic data and individual rating information.

According to an agency official, OCC began to post some limited information on the average size of some performance-based pay increases on the agency intranet in November 2006. The information included the average, agency wide percentage increases for merit increases, merit bonuses, and special act and spot awards, as well as the percentage of employees receiving the increases.

During the performance appraisal cycle we reviewed, OTS shared with union representatives some data on average pay increases. The agency did not share ratings distribution data with the union, and did not make either performance-based pay increase or rating results information available to all employees. However, in November 2006, OTS distributed to all employees information for the recently completed appraisal cycle on the percentage of employees who received each performance rating level and the average pay increase percentages to be received by people at each level. The information was disaggregated by regions and Washington, D.C.

While SEC did not make the results of performance rating decisions available to all employees, officials said that they reported information on performance awards (bonuses) to the union and that, under implementation of the compensation and benefits agreement currently being negotiated, they plan to publish aggregated information on performance ratings under the planned new performance management system for non-executive employees. SEC officials also told us that they plan to provide information at the lowest possible organizational level while still protecting individual confidentiality.

The remaining five financial regulators did not share overall data on ratings or performance increases widely with all employees, although in some cases some information was shared with managers. The following outlines how information was shared:

- CFTC shared information on the results of ratings and award decisions with managers on a Pay Parity Governance Committee, but not with all employees, for the appraisal cycle we reviewed. CFTC officials told us that there is no prohibition against sharing this type of information under the new performance management system directive, and they are aware that there is some interest among employees in receiving it. They said that the pay parity committee will determine whether there is value in releasing this information to all employees in the future.
- At FHFB, an official told us that office directors see all the ratings within their offices and make the decisions about the performance-based pay increases for employees, but this information is not shared across offices or with all employees. However, the director of the Office of Supervision, FHFB's largest office, has shared information with all staff in the office on the ranges of pay increases corresponding to different performance rating levels and base salary levels that were received by staff within the office for a given year, as well as the standards used to assign the merit increase amounts.

- Officials at OFHEO told us that just last year they started sharing information on the results of ratings and pay increase decisions with management, but that they have not yet shared this type of information with all employees.
- FCA officials told us that they do not share aggregate results of the performance rating and pay increase decisions with all employees. They explained that, under a previous administration, in early 2000, an executive summary was prepared and posted that all employees could potentially access, which contained information on the results of ratings and pay increases. However, this information was not broadly disseminated directly to employees.
- NCUA shares information on the results of the merit pay decisions with directors, but not with all employees. An NCUA official told us that it is up to the directors to decide whether or not to share this information with their staff. In comments on the draft report, NCUA explained that this is one of the issues involved in its current negotiations over pay and benefits with the National Treasury Employees Union, and that the agency's proposal to the union does provide for this type of transparency.

Agencies provided a variety of reasons for not sharing overall ratings and pay increase information more widely. Officials from FHFB and FCA told us that the relatively small size of their agencies, 122 and 248 employees, respectively, makes it harder to share this type of information while protecting individual confidentiality and that an FHFB official was not aware of employee demand for this type of information. FCA officials also mentioned that the emphasis in their performance management system is on rating individual employees against the standards, not against other employees and they wanted employees to focus on their individual ratings and performance. According to union representatives at OCC, the union has made multiple requests for data on the results of the performance rating and pay increase decisions but management has declined to share information that would enable the union to, in their words, perform a meaningful independent analysis of the ratings and pay increase decisions. OCC officials told us that they prefer not to share with employees disaggregated information on ratings and pay increase distributions because organizational units administer the process differently. For example, the percentages of individuals rated at the highest level (4) and next highest level (3) vary from unit to unit. Because units receive fixed pools of funds for performance-based increases, the average size of a merit increase that an employee receiving a level 4 may receive can vary from unit to unit, depending on how many individuals receive the highest rating.[23] OCC officials told us that sharing information on average merit increases by unit with employees, without sufficient context of the factors considered when making these decisions, including more detailed rating information (which is privacy protected), could lead to misinterpretation of the data.

However, not sharing information on the results of the performance rating and pay increase decisions processes can detract from the goal of a transparent and fair performance management system. This information needs to be presented in ways that protect individual confidentiality, such as by aggregating it. Without access to this type of information, individual employees can lose a valuable opportunity to understand how their performance stands relative to others in their organization. In cases where agencies negotiate agreements with unions, an important consideration is to reach agreement to share aggregate results of the rating and pay increase decisions with employees, while protecting individual confidentiality.

While Financial Regulators Generally Used Multiple Rating Levels to Make Meaningful Distinctions in Performance, Employees at Most Agencies Were Concentrated in One or Two Rating Categories, with Very Few Poor Performers

While most of the financial regulatory agencies used multiple rating levels to assess employee performance and make distinctions in performance, at most agencies employees were concentrated in one or two rating categories and very few received poor performance ratings. By using multiple-level rating systems, agencies have the capability to make meaningful distinctions in performance. Effective performance management systems make meaningful distinctions between acceptable and outstanding performance of individuals and appropriately reward those who perform at the highest level. As we have previously reported, performance management systems can provide management with the objective and fact-based information it needs to reward top performers and provide the necessary information and documentation to deal with poor performers.[24] More specifically, using multiple rating levels provides a useful framework for making distinctions in performance by allowing an agency to differentiate, at a minimum, between poor, acceptable, and outstanding performance. We have reported that two-level rating systems by definition will generally not provide meaningful distinctions in performance ratings, with possible exceptions for employees in entry-level or developmental bands.[25]

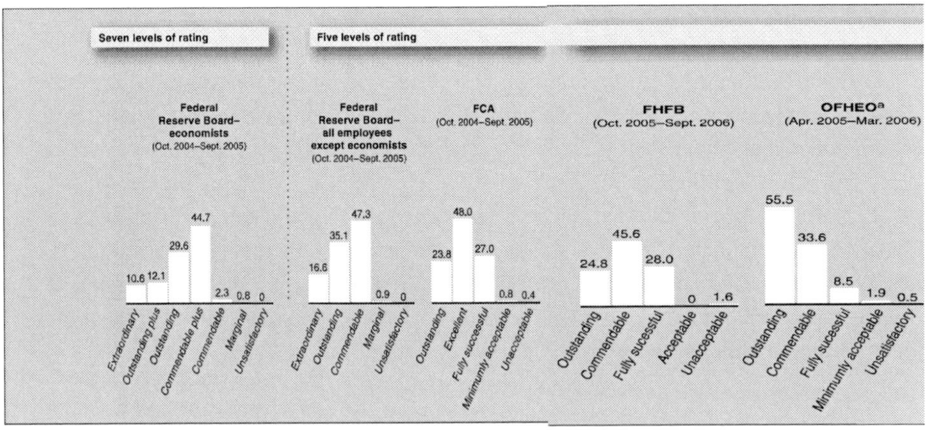

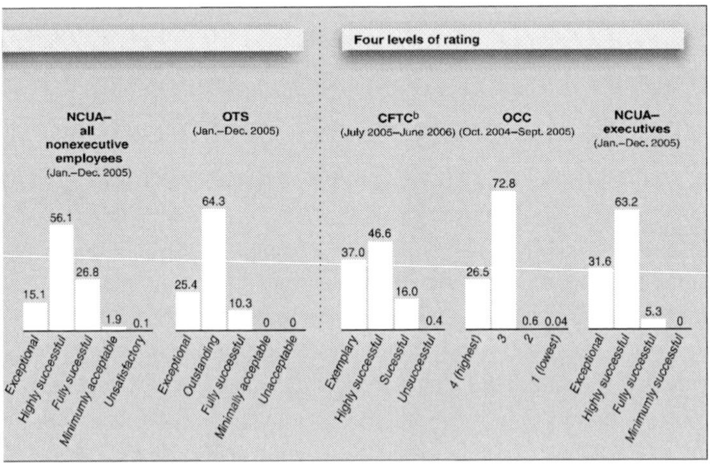

Source: GAO analysis of agency data.

Note: The dates of the performance appraisal cycles varied across agencies, as indicated in this figure and in table 3, appendix I. SEC had two distinct cycles affecting two different groups of employees.

[a]OFHEO distinguished between "high" and "low" level performance scores within rating categories. The percentage values shown in the graphic include employees with scores at both the high and low levels within categories. For example, the percentage value shown in the graphic for the "Outstanding" rating category includes those employees rated as high-level outstanding and low-level outstanding combined. According to OFHEO officials, about 32 percent of employees fell into the low-level outstanding category.

[b]The new CFTC performance management system that went into effect in October 2006 has five rating levels.

Figure 1. Percentage of Regulatory Employees by Rating Level for Systems with Multiple Rating Levels, for Completed Appraisal Cycles Specified.

Eight agencies used four or more rating levels. For example, as described earlier, OFHEO used a five-level rating category system to appraise employee performance and contributions toward achieving agency goals, and further distinguished between high and low performance scores within rating categories. As shown in figure 1, at the eight agencies with four- or five-level rating systems, the largest percentage of employees fell into the second highest rating category, except at OFHEO and the Federal Reserve Board. At OFHEO, more than half of the employees were placed into the high or low levels of the top rating category. Conversely, at the Federal Reserve Board (excluding economists), almost half of the employees fell into the third highest or middle (commendable) rating category. Across the eight agencies shown in figure 1, the percentage of employees who fell into the highest rating category varied from 10.6 percent for economists at the Federal Reserve Board, to 55 percent of employees at OFHEO.

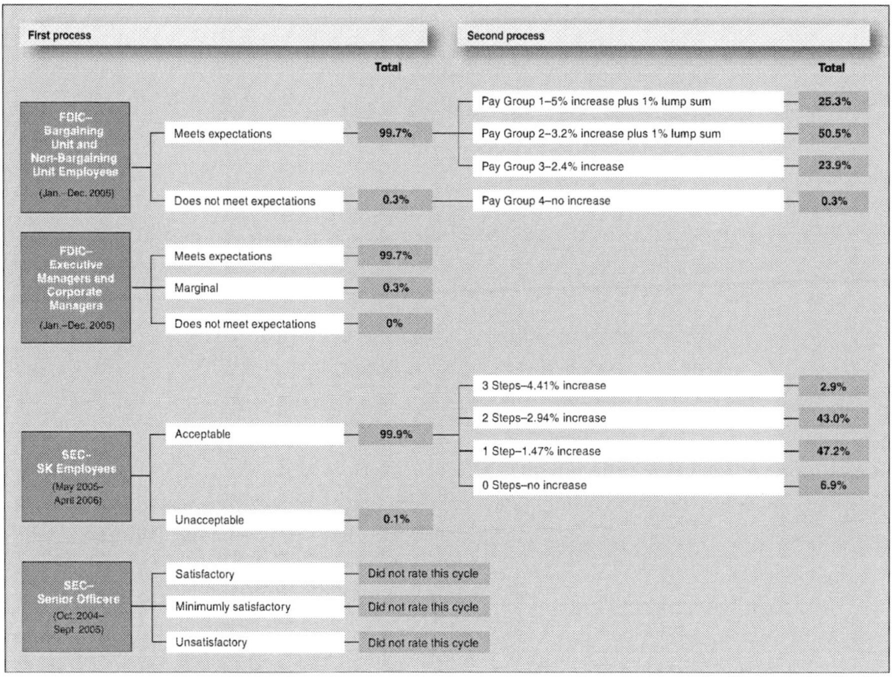

Source: GAO analysis of agency data.

Note: At SEC, senior officers were not rated during this rating cycle because, according to officials, the agency did not have the budget to fund any merit increases. SK employees at SEC include all employees other than senior officers.

Figure 2. Percentage of Regulatory Employees by Rating Level and Merit Increase Category for Agencies with Pass/Fail Performance Rating Systems, for Completed Appraisal Cycles Specified.

SEC and FDIC used two-level rating systems (essentially pass/fail systems) to appraise the performance of certain groups of employees. Although two-level rating systems by definition will not provide meaningful distinctions in performance ratings, both SEC and FDIC used a second process to determine performance-based pay increases and effectively make more meaningful performance distinctions. As figure 2 shows, the highest percentage of employees at FDIC fell into the second highest of four categories, in keeping with the fixed percentages included in the negotiated agreement with the union. At SEC, the largest percentage of employees fell into the third highest of four rating categories.

As shown in figures 1 and 2, the percentage of employees rated as poor performers at each agency was very small during the completed performance appraisal cycles we reviewed. Employees rated at below the successful and meets expectations rating levels accounted for less than 3 percent of employees across the agencies.[26] OTS had zero employees in the bottom two rating categories combined—all OTS employees received fully successful or higher ratings. Similarly at NCUA, no executives and 2.1 percent of non-executives were rated below minimally successful.

While the financial regulators rated very few employees as poor performers, all of the agencies have established procedures to deal with poor performers. When an employee does not perform up to a threshold standard for satisfactory performance, most agencies place the employee on a performance improvement plan or provide counseling for the employee, and the employee does not receive a performance-based increase at the end of the performance cycle. For example, OTS has addressed poor performance by working with the employee to improve his or her area of deficiency. An employee who receives a rating at the unacceptable level is placed on a performance improvement plan for a minimum of 90 days. Specifically, OTS policy advises supervisors to develop a performance improvement plan by identifying the performance areas in which the employee is deficient and the types of improvements, including specific work products and steps to be followed which the employee must complete to attain the fully successful performance level. In addition, according to OTS policy, the agency may provide the employee with closer supervision, or on-the-job or formal training.

However, governmentwide, 29.7 percent of employees indicated in the 2006 Office of Personnel Management (OPM) Federal Human Capital Survey that they agreed or strongly agreed that differences in performance within the work unit were recognized in a meaningful way. Positive responses to this question for the eight financial regulators who participated in the survey ranged from 24.9 percent for CFTC to 41.6 percent for OCC. None of these agencies had a majority of their employees provide positive responses to this question, and only three of the eight agencies had more than one third of their employees provide positive responses to this question.

SEC Did Not Complete Performance Ratings for Senior Officers, Missing an Opportunity to Provide Valuable Feedback

While it may have been an isolated incident, for senior officers, SEC effectively did not make distinctions in rating their performance during the appraisal cycle we reviewed because the agency did not complete performance ratings for them in 2005. According to SEC officials, no funds were available for performance-based bonuses (which are normally dependent on performance ratings) during that assessment cycle. As a result, divisions performed assessments of senior officers, but the assessment process was not completed and their ratings were not signed by the Chairman for the October 1, 2004, to September 30, 2005, performance appraisal cycle. A recent SEC Inspector General report confirmed that senior officers in SEC's Enforcement Division did not prepare performance review documents for the performance cycle that ended on September 30, 2005, and recommended that required steps of the senior officer performance appraisal process be conducted in accordance with Commission policy, even when merit increases are not awarded.[27] All senior officers received annual across-the-board salary increases during that cycle. Conducting performance appraisals and making distinctions in performance are important not only for determining performance-based pay increases, but for providing feedback to help employees improve their performance and assess how their work contributed to achieving organizational goals. By not appraising their performance, SEC missed an opportunity to provide valuable feedback to senior officers.

Agencies Have Taken Various Actions to Seek to Maintain Pay and Benefits Comparability

Financial regulators have hired external compensation consultants to conduct individual, formal comparability surveys, exchanged pay and benefits information, explored the feasibility of conducting a common survey, and adjusted pay and benefits to seek to maintain pay and benefits comparability. The majority of the financial regulators conducted pay comparability surveys that have included other financial regulators and in some instances, private-sector entities. To compare pay across agencies, consultants send questionnaires on behalf of the sponsoring agency and ask participating agencies to match the jobs based on the job descriptions provided. To compare benefits, consultants use various methods, such as side-by-side comparisons of benefits and calculation of total cost of benefits per employee. In addition to these surveys, human capital officials at the 10 financial regulators have formed an interagency group to exchange information and consult on topics such as updates on merit pay ranges and bonuses. However, agency officials told us that because many of the financial regulators conduct separate comparability surveys, their staffs have to respond to numerous and often overlapping inquiries, which can be inefficient. To begin addressing the inefficiencies of this process, the agencies formed a subcommittee in December 2006 to study the feasibility of conducting a common survey on pay and benefits. According to agency officials, the subcommittee also has discussed the feasibility of establishing a Web-based data system to make the most current pay and benefits information available to participating agencies.

In the absence of a legislative definition of what constitutes comparability, agency officials told us that they use various methods to assess pay and benefits comparability after they have obtained relevant data from the other agencies. For example, FDIC has sought to set its total pay ranges (base pay plus locality pay) for specific occupations and grade levels within 10 percent of the average of FIRREA agencies. FCA used the average market rate paid by other financial regulators as a benchmark. Finally, partly on the basis of the results of the comparability surveys and discussions among the agencies, the financial regulators have adjusted their pay and benefits policies in their efforts to seek to maintain comparability. For example, as a result of gaining pay flexibilities, CFTC implemented new pay ranges for its 2003 pay schedule, and increased base pay by 20 percent for all eligible employees to partially close the 25 percent gap between CFTC and FIRREA agencies. Appendix IV provides additional information on our analysis of individual agency actions.

While the regulators have taken actions to seek to maintain comparability in their pay and benefits, there are some variations in base pay ranges and benefit packages among the agencies. Figure 3 shows the base pay ranges (minimum and maximum) for the mission-critical occupations, excluding executives at the 10 agencies.[28] As shown in the same figure, the actual average base pay among the 10 agencies also varies somewhat in relation to the agencies' respective base pay ranges, which according to agency officials, could be affected by the average length of service of employees, and the fact that some agencies tend to hire employees at certain grade levels.

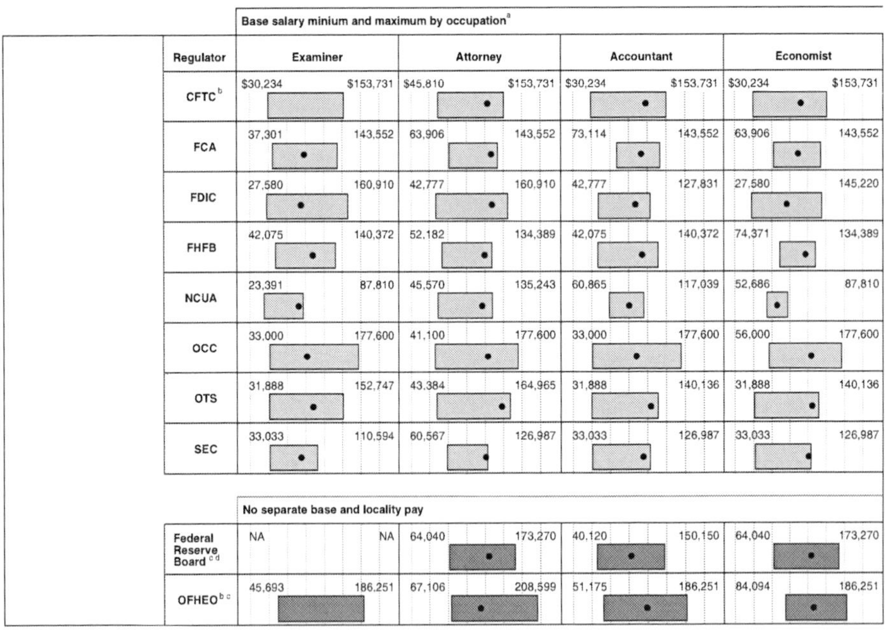

Figure 3. Continued on next page.

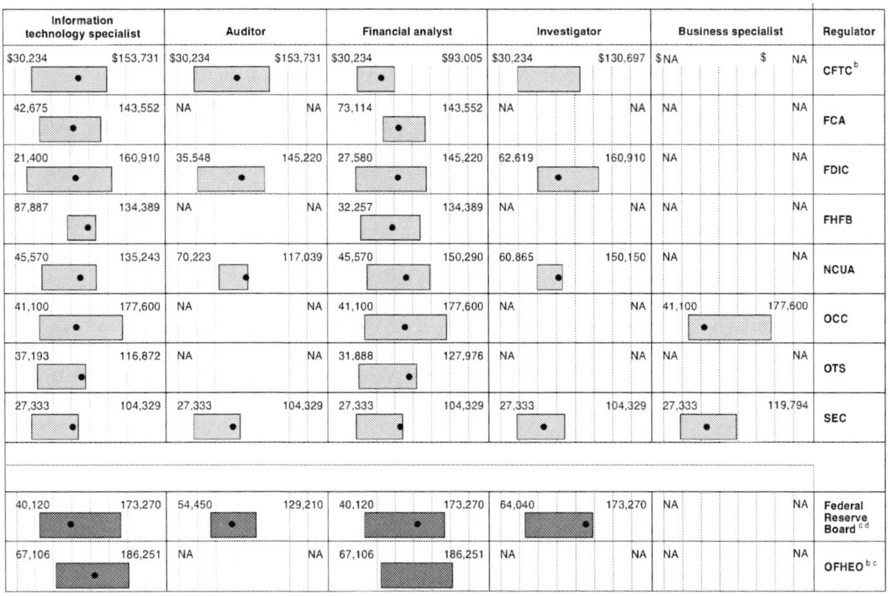

Actual average base pay

Sources: GAO analysis of agency data for pay ranges and Central Personnel Data File data for actual pay.

[a]The figure shows the minimum pay of the lowest level and the maximum pay of the highest level of an occupation for which agencies have an established occupation. Agencies may not currently have incumbents in each level of the occupation. The base pay ranges exclude locality pay except for the Federal Reserve Board and OFHEO.

[b]The actual average base pay data in CPDF did not segregate CFTC's examiners and investigators or OFHEO's examiners and financial analysts because these occupations are assigned the same OPM job series number. Therefore, we did not separately present the actual average pay for these four occupations at the two agencies. The combined actual average pay for examiners and investigators is $8 3,501 at CFTC; and $131,294 for examiners and financial analysts at OFHEO.

[c]The base pay ranges shown for the Federal Reserve Board and OFHEO reflect the agencies' total pay ranges because Washington D.C., is the agencies' only duty station.

[d]The actual average base pay data are provided by the Federal Reserve Board because CPDF does not contain data for the Board.

Figure 3. Non-executive Minimum and Maximum Pay Ranges and Average Actual Pay for Mission-Critical Occupations by Regulator, 2006.

Because each financial regulator sets its own locality pay percentage based on its respective policies, locality pay percentages often differ from those that OPM sets for General Schedule employees (with the exception of CFTC) and vary among agencies for the same duty station. For example, in New York City, the OPM locality pay percentage is 22.97 percent but the regulators' locality pay percentages range from 21.19 at FDIC and FHFB to 33.20 percent at OTS. Table 2 shows the locality pay percentages for OPM and for the eight financial regulators that have locality pay percentages for selected cities.

Table 2. Selected OPM Locality Pay Percentages Compared to Financial Regulators' Locality Pay Percentages, Fiscal Year 2006

Locality	OPM	CFTC	OCC	OTS	FDIC	FCA	FHFB	NCUA	SEC
Atlanta, Ga.	**15.10%**	N/A	N/A	6.50%	7.43%	N/A	7.43%	8.06%	11.13%
Boston, Mass.	**19.99**	N/A	13.00	17.50	22.67 a	N/A	22.67	18.55	24.29
Chicago, Ill.	**21.15**	21.15	8.00	11.20	16.20	N/A	16.20	22.26	21.62
Dallas, Tex.	**16.39**	N/A	3.00	N/A	9.20	6.50	9.20	11.25	12.92
Denver, Colo.	**19.49**	N/A	8.00	2.30	N/A	10.50	N/A	18.27	17.72
Los Angeles, Calif.	**23.18**	N/A	18.00	18.10	19.28	N/A	N/A	25.70	24.35
Miami, Fla.	**17.84**	N/A	3.00	6.80	11.33 b	N/A	N/A	15.97	15.02
Minneapolis, Minn.	**17.31**	17.31	3.00	7.30	11.76	8.20[c]	N/A	13.23	N/A
New York City, N.Y.	**22.97**	22.97	23.00	33.20	21.19	N/A	21.19	23.61	24.92
San Francisco, Calif.	**28.68**	N/A	28.00	46.70	32.41	N/A	32.41	36.43	25.14
Seattle, Wash.	**17.93**	N/A	8.00	15.80	13.93	N/A	13.93	14.52	N/A
Washington, D.C.	**17.50**	17.50	8.00	25.90	13.30	15.20[d]	16.30	12.87	17.50

Source: GAO analysis of agency data.

Note: Washington D.C. is the Federal Reserve Board's and OFHEO's only duty station, thus the agencies do not have separate locality pay percentages. For the other agencies, N/A indicates localities where they had no office.

[a] Locality includes Braintree, Mass.

[b] Locality includes Sunrise, Fla.

[c] Locality includes Bloomington, Minn.

[d] Locality includes McLean, Va.

The benefits that the 10 financial regulators offered also varied, which we discuss in detail in appendix IV. For example, half of the regulators offer their employees 401(k) retirement savings plans with varying employer contributions in addition to offering the governmentwide Federal Thrift Saving Plan (except for the Federal Reserve Board). According to agency officials, factors such as the year an agency first became subject to comparability provisions, budget constraints, the needs and preferences of different workforces, and ways to attract and retain workforces play a role in compensation decisions and contribute to the variations in pay ranges and benefits. Moreover, agency officials emphasized that it was not their goal to have identical pay and benefits packages; rather, they considered pay and benefits as a total package when seeking to maintain pay and benefits comparability and when setting pay policies aimed at recruiting and retaining employees.

FEW EMPLOYEES HAVE MOVED AMONG THE FINANCIAL REGULATORS; MOST RESIGNED FROM FEDERAL EMPLOYMENT

While the total number of financial regulatory employees resigning from federal employment between fiscal years 1990 and 2006 generally declined, there was no clear trend among the number who moved to another financial regulator. As shown in figure 4, the number of employees leaving one federal regulator for another declined from the previous fiscal year in 10 of the 16 years and increased from the previous fiscal year in the other 6 years. Figure 4 also shows the percentage of financial regulatory employees who went to another financial regulator, went to other federal agencies, and resigned from federal employment, and the total number of financial regulatory employees during this period. Of all the employees who left their financial regulatory agency voluntarily (moved to another financial regulator or executive branch agency, or resigned) from fiscal year 1990 through fiscal year 2006, the vast majority—86 percent (13,433)—of the 15,627 employees leaving the regulators voluntarily (i.e., moved or resigned), resigned from the federal government. The number of employees who moved to another financial regulator ranged from a low of 16 of 1,362 who moved or resigned in fiscal year 1997 to a high of 97 of 1,229 who moved or resigned in fiscal year 1991. The total number of financial regulator employees was 15,400 and 19,796 during those 2 years, respectively.[29] Similar lows were also experienced in 1996 and 2003. Some agency officials told us that they believe that the FIRREA comparability provision and similar provisions in subsequent laws applicable to financial regulators have been effective in ensuring that regulators' pay and benefits are generally comparable among the 10 agencies, which probably helps minimize employee movement among financial regulatory agencies. Of the financial regulator employees who moved or resigned, the percentage of those who resigned from federal employment fluctuated slightly over the period, ranging from a low of 73.7 percent in fiscal year 2003 to a high of 94.8 percent in fiscal year 1996.

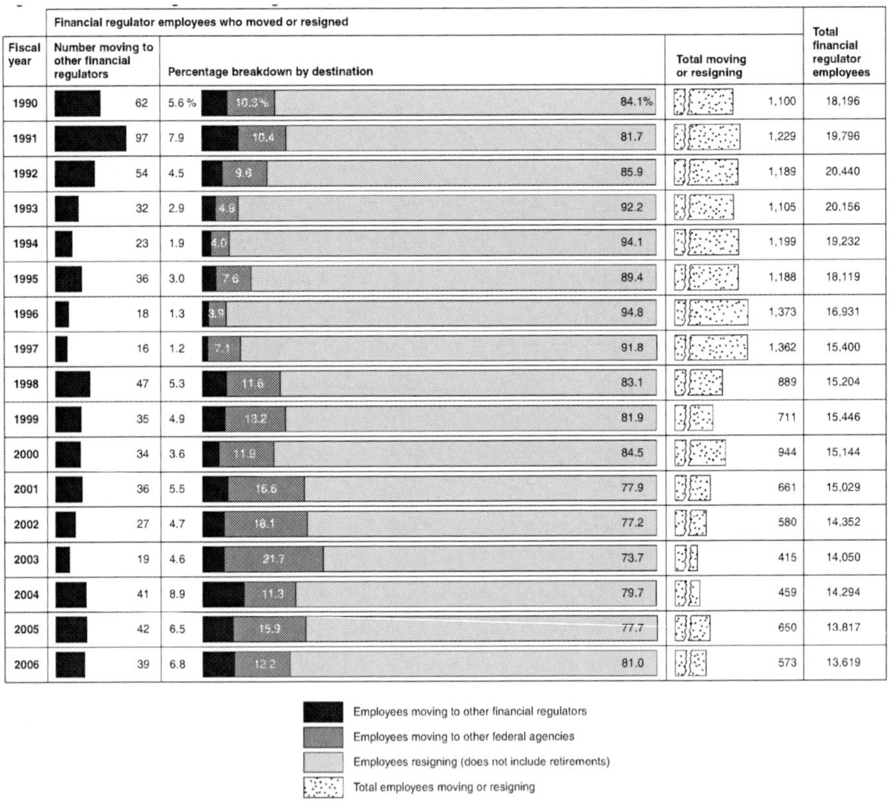

Source: GAO analysis of CPDF data.
Note: This figure does not include data for the Federal Reserve Board.

Figure 4. Attrition among Financial Regulators, Fiscal Years 1990–2006.

The movement of mission-critical employees among financial regulators also did not reveal a discernible trend. For the number of employees who moved to another financial regulator from fiscal year 1990 through fiscal year 2006, see table 10 in appendix V. The numbers ranged from no movement for 7 of the 11 occupational categories (accountants, auditors, business specialists, economists, financial analysts, investigators, and information technology (IT) specialists) in at least 1 of the fiscal years we reviewed to a high of 37 employees (38.1 percent of all those who moved that fiscal year) for the "all other" occupational category in fiscal year 1991.[30] During this period (fiscal years 1990 to 2006), some occupational categories experienced very little movement. For example, fewer accountants, auditors, business specialists, and investigators moved than employees in the other categories. In contrast, examiners had the largest number of employees moving among financial regulators in 8 of the 17 years, including the 3 most recent years for which data were available. The average number of employees in mission-critical occupations moving among the 9 financial regulators from fiscal year 1990 through fiscal year 2006 ranged from 0.1 for investigators to 11.7 for examiners. See appendix V for additional data on employee movement.

For those employees that did not move to another financial regulator, we could not determine in all cases where the employees moved because CPDF, the most complete data set available with federal employment information, does not include information on employment outside executive branch agencies. We were able to identify those employees that went to another federal agency. These numbers ranged from a low of 48 in fiscal year 1994 to a high of 128 in fiscal year 1991, higher than the number of employees who moved to another financial regulator, which was 23 in fiscal year 1994 and 97 in fiscal year 1991. Officials from the 9 agencies told us that they do not track the employment of their employees after the employees leave their agencies. Further, they said that their employees generally sought employment outside the federal government, including the private sector and state and local government, but that their main competitors were private-sector entities.

CONCLUSIONS

Like other federal agencies, the experiences of the financial regulators illustrate the challenges inherent in establishing well-functioning, performance-based pay systems and that these systems are works in progress that are constantly evolving. These regulators have taken various approaches to revise their performance management systems and introduce performance-based pay. Although the regulators have incorporated many of the key practices for effective performance management systems, opportunities exist for a number of them to make improvements as they continue to refine their systems. Specifically, some regulators have opportunities in the areas of strengthening safeguards to enhance transparency and fairness and making meaningful distinctions in performance. As some regulators develop new systems or revise their existing systems, they have an opportunity to build in aspects of the key practices, such as improving transparency by communicating the overall results of performance appraisal rating and performance-based pay increase decisions to all employees to help employees understand how they performed relative to other employees in their organization, while protecting individual confidentiality. For regulators that negotiate with unions, there are also opportunities to work together to accomplish this.

SEC has some additional opportunities to pursue improvements in specific aspects of its performance management system, which it is in the process of revamping. For example, SEC can establish and communicate to non-executive employees using the new system clear criteria for making performance rating and pay increase decisions. Finally, while it may have been an isolated incident, by not completing performance assessments of senior officers in the 2005 performance appraisal cycle we reviewed, SEC missed an opportunity for two-way feedback and assessments of individual and organizational progress toward organizational goals. While funding circumstances specific to that appraisal cycle contributed to this situation, in the future it will be important to complete assessments regardless of the availability of funding for increases.

The agencies have taken a variety of actions in seeking to maintain pay and benefits comparability. While we did find some variation in base pay ranges, locality pay percentages, actual average pay, and benefits among the agencies, we found that a number of reasons could contribute to the variation, including the following: regulators were granted flexibility under Title V and subject to comparability requirements at varying times, pay and benefits are considered comprehensively in seeking comparability, the average length of service of employees, and where employees are located.

While pay and benefits comparability cannot be precisely determined, all the agencies are working to maintain comparability in pay and benefits. One recent initiative—studying the feasibility of conducting a common survey on pay and benefits—should help to increase the efficiency of this effort. In addition, given the relatively small amount of employee movement among federal regulators, the variation in pay, benefits, and locality pay percentages in some locations across the regulators does not appear to be encouraging large numbers of employees to move among financial regulators. This may be an indication that the comparability provisions of FIRREA and other pertinent legislation have been working as intended. Moreover, from fiscal years 1990 through 2006, the agencies' attrition rates have trended downward indicating that a smaller percentage of employees were leaving.

APPENDIX I. OBJECTIVES, SCOPE, AND METHODOLOGY

The objectives of this report were to (1) review how the performance-based pay systems of 10 federal financial regulatory agencies are aligned with six key practices for effective performance management systems, (2) review actions these 10 agencies have taken to assess and implement comparability in compensation, and (3) review the extent to which individuals in selected occupations have moved between or left any of the agencies. These agencies are the Commodity Futures Trading Commission (CFTC), the Farm Credit Administration (FCA), the Federal Deposit Insurance Corporation (FDIC), the Federal Housing Finance Board (FHFB), the Board of Governors of the Federal Reserve System (the Federal Reserve Board), the National Credit Union Administration (NCUA), the Office of the Comptroller of the Currency (OCC), the Office of Federal Housing Enterprise Oversight (OFHEO), the Office of Thrift Supervision (OTS), and the Securities and Exchange Commission (SEC).

To address our first objective, we analyzed documents on the regulators' performance management and pay systems, including guidance, policies, and procedures on the systems; performance planning and appraisal forms; union contracts and agreements; training materials; internal evaluations of systems; and materials used to communicate with employees about the systems. We also reviewed documents assessing the agencies' systems, including results from the 2006 Federal Human Capital Survey conducted by the Office of Personnel Management (OPM), recent human resources operations audits performed by OPM, and relevant material from agencies' offices of inspector general.

We also interviewed key human resources officials at each agency, as well as officials from other functional areas knowledgeable about each agency's performance-based pay practices. In addition, we interviewed employees at the agencies who served as members of employee groups. At six of the agencies, the employees we spoke with were union representatives. Specifically, employees at FDIC, OCC, NCUA, and SEC are represented by the National Treasury Employees Union, and OTS headquarters staff and CFTC staff at two regional offices are represented by the American Federation of Government Employees. Employees at FCA, the Federal Reserve Board, FHFB, and OFHEO did not have a union; at these agencies we spoke with employees who served on employee committees or working groups.

Table 3. Performance Appraisal Cycle by Agency

Agency	Performance appraisal cycle
CFTC	July 1, 2005 to June 30, 2006
FCA	October 1, 2004 to September 30, 2005
FDIC	January 1, 2005 to December 31, 2005
Federal Reserve Board	October 1, 2004 to September 30, 2005
FHFB	October 1, 2005 to September 30, 2006
NCUA	January 1, 2005 to December 31, 2005
OCC	October 1, 2004 to September 30, 2005
OFHEO	April 1, 2005 to March 31, 2006
OTS	January 1, 2005 to December 31, 2005
SEC:	
for senior officers	October 1, 2004 to September 30, 2005
for all other employees	May 1, 2005 to April 30, 2006

Source: Various regulators.

In addition, we examined small, select sets of individual performance plans for employees, which outline the annual performance expectations for employees. The selection of these performance plans was not intended to allow us to make generalizations about all performance plans at the agencies, and we have used information from the plans for illustrative purposes only. The performance plans we received were selected by agency officials based on our request for a mix of occupations and grade levels at each agency. The smallest number of performance plans we examined from an agency was one, in a case where the performance plans for all employees are completely standardized. The largest number of plans we reviewed from an agency was 32. The individual performance plans we examined pertained to each agency's last completed performance appraisal cycle when we began this review. Table 3 shows the appraisal cycle by agency.

Finally, we analyzed data from each agency on performance ratings and performance-based pay awarded to employees as well as aggregate data on all types of pay increases at each agency not linked to performance ratings. We used these data to calculate the Spearman rank correlation coefficient to show the strength of the relationship between employee performance ratings and the associated performance-based percentage pay increases at each agency.[1] In computing the correlation coefficients, we noted that a few agencies used a table or procedure that specified particular pay increases corresponding to specific ratings. Taken in isolation, the use of the table or procedure would be expected to produce a perfect correlation, i.e., +1.0. However, other aspects of these agencies' systems contributed to the resulting coefficients being less than +1.0. For example, at one agency, employees with rating scores below a certain threshold were not eligible for any pay increase. While these employees may have had different rating scores, none of them received a pay increase, which contributed to a coefficient that was less than perfect. Other mechanistic factors in these agencies' systems, such as adjusting or changing the specified percentage pay increase based on the grade level or current salary of the employee, also had the effect of producing a less than perfect coefficient at these agencies. Given the influence that these procedural but nondiscretionary variations may have had on the resulting coefficients at these agencies, the coefficients are primarily useful in their overall demonstration of the positive linkage between ratings and pay increases at all the agencies, and the range of coefficients that occurs. The magnitude of the coefficients, however, is not sufficient for ranking the agencies or making other types of comparisons.

We also analyzed agency data on performance ratings to determine the distribution of employee performance ratings at each agency. All data were provided to us by agency officials, and pertained to the performance appraisal cycles noted in table 3.

To address our second objective, we first analyzed the content of compensation comparability provisions in the agencies' laws and related legislative histories. We reviewed the most recent pay and benefits surveys conducted by external compensation consultants for these agencies, obtained agency pay and benefits data, and analyzed actual pay data from CPDF. In addition, we interviewed agency officials about their experience with these surveys and the agencies' informal interactions to assess pay comparability and to determine the feasibility of conducting a common survey.

To report on the pay ranges for non-executive employees in selected occupations, we analyzed the base pay data provided to us for mission- critical occupations at nine of the agencies in our review. We selected the mission critical occupations by: (1) identifying non-clerical and non-blue-collar occupations with 45 or more employees in at least one financial regulatory agency and (2) vetting this list with the 10 agencies.[2] The agencies provided us with pay range information as set forth in each agency's pay policies as of September 2006 for every job title under each occupational category, including jobs with no incumbents at the time the agencies reported the data to us.

To report on the actual average base pay of employees in the selected occupations, we analyzed actual pay data from CPDF for fiscal year 2006. Because the CPDF does not include data for all agencies, the Federal Reserve Board provided us with actual pay data for our analysis of its employees' actual average pay for fiscal year 2006. To show the financial regulators' locality pay percentages and general schedule employees' locality pay percentages, we selected the cities where four or more financial regulators had duty stations in fiscal year 2006. We obtained fiscal year 2006 locality pay percentages information from the financial regulators and general schedule locality pay percentages from the OPM Web site. To report on the benefits offered by the agencies, we obtained and analyzed data from each agency that included a list of benefits the financial regulators offered as of September 2006 and brief descriptions of each benefit. We also interviewed agency officials about the factors that affect the actual average base pay, and how each agency sets its locality pay percentage.

To address our third objective, we analyzed movement data from CPDF for fiscal years 1990 to 2006, the most recent available data as of December 2006. For each fiscal year, we identified the number of employees in selected mission-critical occupations at a financial regulator who (1) moved to another financial regulator, (2) moved to other federal agencies, and (3) resigned from federal employment. We identified those who moved from one financial regulatory agency to another by identifying employees who had a CPDF separation code for a voluntary transfer and who also had a CPDF accession code from another financial regulatory agency within 25 days of the transfer out. Also, for each mission-critical occupation, we examined the number of financial regulator employees who moved to another financial regulator in each fiscal year and the average number of employees who moved among the nine financial regulators over the 16 years of our review. Our analysis of supervisors included executives, who constituted 1 to 2 percent of all supervisors who moved to another financial regulator. We also included all other agency occupations that were not classified as "mission-critical occupations" in an "all other" category, which includes occupations such as specialists in human resources management, administration, clerical, management and program analysis, blue collar occupations, financial administration, and paralegal work.

We did not include the Federal Reserve Board in our analysis of the movement of financial regulator employees because CPDF does not include data on the Federal Reserve Board. Federal Reserve Board officials told us that data on employee movement for fiscal years 1990 to 1996 are not readily accessible. The agency provided us some data for fiscal years 1997 to 2005, including data on employees who transferred, resigned, were fired, were subject to a reduction in force, or otherwise separated, and the agency's total number of employees, but was unable to identify whether their employees left for another financial regulator. Because the data the agency provided were not comparable with the CPDF data we used for the other financial regulators, we did not include the Federal Reserve Board in our analysis. We also did not include information on the employment of financial regulatory employees after they left federal employment because CPDF does not include data on employment outside some agencies and officials told us that they do not track the employment of their employees after the employees leave their agencies.[3]

We assessed the reliability of the various sets of data used in our study. To assess the reliability of the performance and pay increase data provided by the agencies, we conducted various inspections and electronic testing of the data for reasonableness and the presence of any obvious or potential errors in accuracy and completeness. We also reviewed related agency documentation, interviewed agency officials knowledgeable about the data, and brought to the attention of these officials any concerns or discrepancies we found with the data for correction or updating. Based on the results of these procedures, we believe the data are sufficiently reliable for use in the analyses presented in this report. We did not independently verify the pay and benefits data we received from the agencies but consider these data sufficiently reliable for the illustrative purpose of our review. Based on our data reliability testing of CPDF data, we believe the CPDF data are sufficiently reliable for this review. When analyzing employee movement using CPDF data, we found exceptions from standard personnel procedures, such as employees with a transfer-out code but with an accession code in the hiring agency that was not a transfer-in code, or employee records with transfer-out and transfer-in dates that exceeded 3 calendar days. We also found duplicate separation or accession records for the same individual on the same day. We deleted one of the duplicate records. We also found cases where an individual had two separation actions on the same day but they were different types of actions (e.g., a transfer out and a resignation). Because we could not determine which separation action was the correct one, we deleted both records. However, these types of data problems represented less than one-tenth of 1 percent of the data used. As a result, we concluded that the data were sufficiently reliable to show the magnitude of movement between financial regulatory agencies, to other federal agencies, and to nonfederal employers.

We conducted our work from February 2006 through June 2007 in accordance with generally accepted government auditing standards.

Appendix II. Information on Agencies

Table 4. Agency Information

Agency	Mission	Number of employees[a]	Funding[b]	Employee representation	Performance-based pay
Commodity Futures Trading Commission (CFTC)	To protect market users and the public from fraud, manipulation, and abusive practices related to the sale of commodity and financial futures and options, and to foster open, competitive, and financially sound commodity futures and option markets.	446	Appropriated	The American Federation of Government Employees represents employees in CFTC's Chicago and New York offices only.	In October 2006, CFTC began transitioning to a new performance- based pay system that will be fully implemented beginning in July 2007.[c]
Farm Credit Administration (FCA)	To promote a safe, sound, and dependable source of credit and related services for agriculture and rural America.	248	Non-appropriated[d]	FCA is not unionized. FCA has an employee council.	Performance-based pay began in 1993; the system has had some revisions since its inception.
Federal Deposit Insurance Corporation (FDIC)	To maintain stability and public confidence in the nation's financial system by insuring deposits, examining and supervising financial institutions, and managing receiverships.	4328	Non-appropriated	The National Treasury Employees Union has the right to bargain over employees' pay and benefits at FDIC.	Performance-based pay began in 1998. FDIC has essentially two pay and performance management systems - - one that applied to senior managers, and one that applied to bargaining unit employees as well as nonbargaining unit employees.[e]

Table 4. (Continued)

Agency	Mission	Number of employees[a]	Funding[b]	Employee representation	Performance-based pay
Federal Housing Finance Board (FHFB)	To ensure that the 12 federal home loan banks are safe and sound so they serve as a reliable source of liquidity and funding for the nation's housing finance and community investment needs.	122	Non-appropriated	FHFB is not unionized. FHFB has an employee working group.	The performance- based pay system began in the mid 1990s; the system has been slightly revised since its inception.
Board of Governors of the Federal Reserve System	To foster the stability, integrity, and efficiency of the nation's monetary, financial, and payment systems so as to promote optimal macroeconomic performance.	1855	Non-appropriated	The Board is not unionized. The Board has an employee representative committee.	The performance- based pay system began in 1989; the system has been slightly revised since its inception.
National Credit Union Administration (NCUA)	To facilitate the availability of credit union services to all eligible consumers, especially those of modest means, through a regulatory environment that fosters a safe and sound federally insured credit union system.	919	Non-appropriated	The National Treasury Employees Union has the right to bargain over the impact and implementation of changes made to NCUA's performance management system.	The performance- based pay system began in 1991.

Table 4. (Continued on next page.)

Agency	Mission	Number of employees[a]	Funding[b]	Employee representation	Performance-based pay
Office of the Comptroller of the Currency (OCC) U.S. Department of the Treasury	The OCC was created by Congress to charter national banks, to oversee a nationwide system of banking institutions, and to assure that national banks are safe and sound, competitive and profitable, and capable of serving in the best possible manner the banking needs of their customers.	2908	Non-appropriated	The National Treasury Employees Union has the right to bargain over the impact and implementation of changes made to OCC's performance management system, but not over employee pay and benefits.	Performance-based pay began in 1981; the current performance management system began in 2001, although some revisions have been made since then.
Office Of Federal Housing Enterprise Oversight (OFHEO)	To promote housing and a strong economy by ensuring the safety and soundness of Fannie Mae and Freddie Mac and fostering the strength and vitality of the nation's housing finance system.	204	Non-appropriated[d]	OFHEO is not unionized. OFHEO has established an ad hoc employee working group.	Performance-based pay has existed since the agency's inception in 1992.

Table 4. (Continued)

Agency	Mission	Number of employees[a]	Funding[b]	Employee representation	Performance-based pay
Office of Thrift Supervision (OTS) U.S. Department of the Treasury	To supervise savings associations and their holding companies in order to maintain their safety and soundness and compliance with consumer laws, and to encourage a competitive industry that meets America's financial services needs.	956	Non-appropriated	The American Federation of Government Employees represents some employees in OTS's Washington, D.C., office only.	Performance-based pay began in 1991.
Securities and Exchange Commission (SEC)	To maintain fair, orderly, and efficient securities markets, facilitate capital formation, and protect investors.	3488	Appropriated	The National Treasury Employees Union represents two- thirds of SEC employees.	Performance-based pay began in 2002.

Source: Various regulators

[a]Employment figure for the Federal Reserve Board is from December 2006 and includes all regular employees; employment figures for all other agencies are for career employees and come from the CPDF as of September 2006.

[b]Some financial regulators receive funding through appropriations from Congress while others are funded from fees collected from members or assessed on regulated entities.

[c]CFTC did not have a performance-based pay system prior to October 2006.

[d]The business operations of FCA and OFHEO are not financed by taxpayer funds. Their annual operating budgets, however, undergo the federal budgetary and appropriations process and are constrained by the amount approved by Congress and signed into law by the President.

[e]The nonbargaining unit employees are never "covered" by the compensation agreement with the union, but rather, the FDIC Board proactively decides annually what performance management and performance-based pay standards will apply to this population. During the performance appraisal cycle we reviewed, the same system that applied to bargaining unit employees was applied to nonbargaining unit employees.

APPENDIX III. FINANCIAL REGULATORS HAVE IMPLEMENTED KEY PRACTICES IN VARYING WAYS

High-performing organizations have recognized that a critical success factor in fostering a results-oriented culture is a performance management system that creates a "line of sight" showing how team, unit, and individual performance can contribute to overall organizational goals and helping employees understand the connection between their daily activities and the organization's success. Effective performance management systems are essential for successfully implementing performance-based pay. In the letter, we addressed important aspects of how 10 financial regulatory agencies have implemented two key practices: (1) linking pay to performance and (2) making meaningful distinctions in performance. This appendix provides detailed information on the financial regulators' implementation of four additional key practices important for effective performance management systems, as well as some additional material pertaining to the linking pay to performance practice covered in the letter. The four additional practices are:

- Align individual performance expectations with organizational goals.
- Connect performance expectations to crosscutting goals.
- Use competencies to provide a fuller assessment of performance.
- Involve employees and stakeholders to gain ownership of performance management systems.

The 10 financial regulatory agencies have implemented these four key practices for effective performance management systems in various ways, reflecting the unique needs of their organizational cultures and structures.

Agencies Have Aligned Individual Performance Expectations with Organizational Goals in Different Ways

The 10 federal financial regulatory agencies have implemented the practice of alignment in a variety of ways. An explicit alignment of daily activities with broader results is a key feature of effective performance management systems in high-performing organizations. These organizations use their performance management systems to improve performance by helping individuals see the connection between their daily activities and organizational goals and encouraging individuals to focus on their roles and responsibilities in helping to achieve these goals. The financial regulators reinforced alignment of individual performance expectations to organizational goals in policy and guidance documents for their performance management systems, used standardized performance elements or standards for employees in their performance plans, used customized individual performance expectations that contributed to organizational goals in individual performance plans, and included the corresponding organizational goals directly on the individual performance plan forms.[1]

Agencies Have Reinforced Alignment in Policies and Guidance for Performance Management Systems

Several of the financial regulatory agencies, including FDIC, OCC, FHFB, and OFHEO, have reinforced alignment by including language on linking individual performance expectations to organizational goals in policy and guidance materials for the performance management systems. The following are examples of how selected agencies have reinforced alignment through policies and guidance.

- A key objective of FDIC's performance management program as stated in a policy directive is to "establish fair and equitable performance expectations and goals for individuals that are tied to accomplishing the organization's mission and objectives."[2] The directive further states that employees at FDIC are assessed against performance criteria, which are defined as "the major goals, objectives, and/or primary responsibilities of a position which contribute toward accomplishing overall organizational goals and objectives" (as found in FDIC's strategic plan and annual performance plan).
- At OCC, the *Policies and Procedures Manual* for the performance management system states that the system is designed to align employee performance expectations with organizational objectives and priorities. The

manual also explains that the starting point for identifying individual performance expectations should be unit objectives established at the executive committee, district, field office, or division level.

- The handbook and guide for FHFB's and OFHEO's performance management systems, respectively, contain several references to alignment of individual expectations to organizational goals.

Agencies Have Included Alignment in Standardized Performance Elements for Employees

Several of the financial regulators, including FCA, CFTC, FHFB, OCC and OTS, have reinforced alignment by including standardized performance elements or performance standards that link performance expectations to organizational goals in employees' performance plans. We have previously reported that results-oriented performance agreements can be effective mechanisms to define accountability for specific goals and to align daily activities with results.[3] Individuals from the agencies with standardized performance elements in their individual performance plans are assessed against the same set of performance elements and standards at the end of the appraisal cycle, as the following examples illustrate.

- FCA has included a requirement to contribute to the achievement of organizational goals in standardized performance elements for all employees in their individual performance plans. Specifically, FCA has developed a set of standardized performance elements for each of its four occupational groups and in some of these elements, requires individuals to contribute to achieving organizational goals and objectives. For the senior manager's occupational group, individuals have a standardized performance element—"Leadership and Motivation Skills"—in their individual performance plans that measures the employees' ability to accomplish the agency's goals and objectives. For the other three occupational groups, individuals have a standardized performance element—"Teamwork and Interpersonal Skills"—in their individual performance plans that measures the extent to which the employee places emphasis on achieving organizational and team goals. In this way, all employees at FCA are assessed on the extent to which they contribute to organizational objectives through a standardized performance element.
- While not requiring a standardized performance element related to alignment in the individual performance plans for all employees, CFTC has reinforced alignment through the performance standards used for rating all employees at the end of the performance appraisal cycle. Specifically, in order for all

employees to achieve the highest summary performance rating, individuals must "achieve element objectives with extensive impact on organizational mission," which reinforces the line of sight between individual performance and organizational results. In this way, for all employees at CFTC, the individual's contributions to organizational goals affect his or her ability to achieve the highest possible performance rating. Alignment is further reinforced for managerial employees at CFTC because they are also assessed on the standardized performance element of "Effective Leadership," which requires them to, among other things, accomplish the mission and organizational goals of the work unit, and communicate organizational goals to subordinates.

- FHFB has reinforced alignment in standardized performance elements for several occupational groups. Standardized elements for executives, managers/supervisors, staff attorneys, and professional positions contain references to aligning with or contributing to organizational goals.
- OCC has applied an alignment focus in a generic performance standard for four occupational groups at the agency. Executives, managers, commissioned examiners, and specialists are all rated against a standardized performance standard that requires them to contribute to organizational goals in order to get the highest rating level of 4 for a particular performance element. For example, managers have a standardized performance element called "leadership skills," for which the highest level performance standard includes language on meeting OCC goals and objectives. Commissioned examiners and specialists have a standardized performance element in their individual performance plans called "organizational skills," with an accompanying performance standard that requires individuals' work products to be closely aligned with OCC's goals, objectives, and priorities in order to receive the highest rating level.
- OTS has reinforced alignment in a standardized performance element for managers and senior managers. Under the "Leadership Skills" standardized performance element, managers are assessed on accomplishing the agency's goals and objectives, taking initiative and incorporating organizational objectives into the organization, and scheduling work assignments. In addition, senior managers have a supplemental performance element that holds them responsible for supporting the achievement of OTS's strategic plan. An OTS official stated that the agency is considering expanding the requirement for alignment as it makes future changes to the performance management system.

Agencies Have Strengthened Alignment by Linking Customized Individual Performance Expectations to Organizational Goals

Several financial regulatory agencies, including SEC, OCC, and the Federal Reserve Board, have reinforced alignment for some individual employees through customized performance expectations specific to individuals that link to higher organizational goals. We have reported that high-performing organizations use their performance management systems to improve performance by helping individuals see the connection between their daily activities and organizational goals and encouraging individuals to focus on their roles and responsibilities to help achieve these goals. One way to encourage this is to align performance expectations of individual employees with organizational goals in individual performance plans. We reviewed a small, select set of individual performance plans from each agency, and identified the following examples of individual performance expectations that linked to higher organizational goals.

- The performance plan for a senior officer at SEC included the performance expectation "Plans and Coordinates Inspection Programs and Ensures that Internal Management Controls Exist and Operate Effectively" that supports SEC's strategic goal to "Maximize the Use of SEC Resources."
- In individual performance plans, OCC has used customized performance expectations unique to the individual in addition to standardized performance elements to appraise employees. Specifically, the performance plan for an information technology (IT) specialist included a customized expectation to provide timely, professional, and quality IT support to promote efficient utilization of OCC resources. This expectation supported the annual OCC objective—"OCC reflects an efficient and effective organization."
- At the Federal Reserve Board, a performance plan for an economist contained a performance expectation to produce a weekly monitoring report on Japan and cover Japanese banking and financial issues, which contributed to one of the Board's annual performance objectives in the area of monetary policy function: "contribute to the development of U.S. international policies and procedures, in cooperation with the U.S. Department of the Treasury and other agencies."

Agencies Have Strengthened Alignment by Stating Organizational Goals in Individual Performance Plans

FHFB and OCC have reinforced the linkage between the individual's performance expectations and organizational goals by including the corresponding organizational goals directly on the individual performance plan forms. This helps make clear the line of sight between the employee's work and agency goals, as the following examples illustrate.

- FHFB has included the agency mission statement and office mission statement to which an employee is contributing at the top of the first page of the performance plan form.

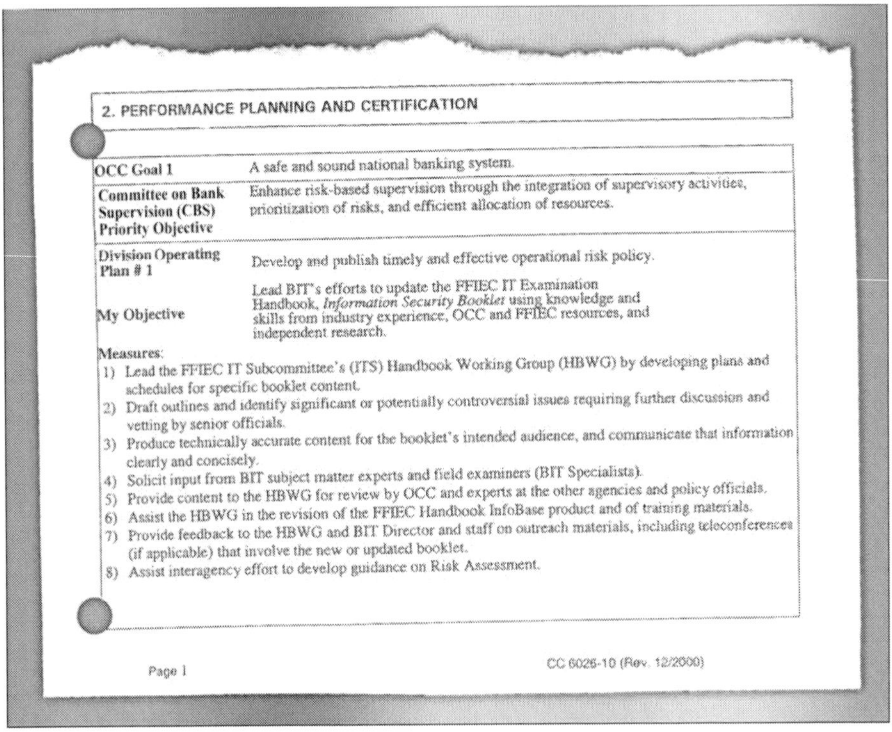

2. PERFORMANCE PLANNING AND CERTIFICATION

OCC Goal 1	A safe and sound national banking system.
Committee on Bank Supervision (CBS) Priority Objective	Enhance risk-based supervision through the integration of supervisory activities, prioritization of risks, and efficient allocation of resources.
Division Operating Plan # 1	Develop and publish timely and effective operational risk policy.
My Objective	Lead BIT's efforts to update the FFIEC IT Examination Handbook, *Information Security Booklet* using knowledge and skills from industry experience, OCC and FFIEC resources, and independent research.

Measures:

1) Lead the FFIEC IT Subcommittee's (ITS) Handbook Working Group (HBWG) by developing plans and schedules for specific booklet content.
2) Draft outlines and identify significant or potentially controversial issues requiring further discussion and vetting by senior officials.
3) Produce technically accurate content for the booklet's intended audience, and communicate that information clearly and concisely.
4) Solicit input from BIT subject matter experts and field examiners (BIT Specialists).
5) Provide content to the HBWG for review by OCC and experts at the other agencies and policy officials.
6) Assist the HBWG in the revision of the FFIEC Handbook InfoBase product and of training materials.
7) Provide feedback to the HBWG and BIT Director and staff on outreach materials, including teleconferences (if applicable) that involve the new or updated booklet.
8) Assist interagency effort to develop guidance on Risk Assessment.

Page 1 CC 6026-10 (Rev. 12/2000)

Source: OCC document; GAO annotation.

Figure 5. Excerpt from an OCC Commissioned Examiner's Individual Performance Plan.

- In many of the individual performance plans we examined from OCC, the annual OCC objective to which each customized performance element contributed was listed on the form, along with performance measures. According to an official, while OCC's performance management policy does not specifically require that the higher organizational objective to which each customized performance element contributes be listed on the employee's performance evaluation form, managers are advised to include the organizational goals and the majority of forms do include them. The official stated that it was an oversight not to include this requirement in the policy, and they plan to revise the performance evaluation form to include space for the corresponding organizational objectives. Figure 5 shows an example of how a customized performance element on an individual performance plan is linked to an agency goal, clarifying the relationship between individual and organizational performance.

AGENCIES HAVE CONNECTED PERFORMANCE EXPECTATIONS TO CROSSCUTTING GOALS IN DIFFERENT WAYS

The financial regulatory agencies have connected performance expectations to crosscutting goals in several ways. As public sector organizations shift their focus of accountability from outputs to results, they have recognized that the activities needed to achieve those results often transcend specific organizational boundaries. We reported that key characteristics of high-performing organizations are collaboration, interaction, and teamwork across organizational boundaries.[4] High-performing organizations use their performance management systems to strengthen accountability for results, specifically by placing greater emphasis on those characteristics fostering the necessary collaboration, both within and across organizational boundaries, to achieve results.

The specific ways in which the financial regulatory agencies have connected performance expectations to crosscutting goals vary. In our review of a small, select set of performance plans from some of the agencies, we identified some examples of customized individual performance plans that identified crosscutting goals that would require collaboration to achieve, as well as either the internal or external organizations with which the individuals would collaborate to achieve those goals. All of the agencies recognized the importance of collaboration by including performance elements for collaboration or teamwork within and across organizational boundaries in individual performance plans for at least some employees. Several agencies applied standardized performance elements related to teamwork or collaboration to employees.

Agencies Have Identified Crosscutting Goals and Organizations for Collaboration in Individual Performance Plans

We found examples of performance plans customized to individuals at OCC, FCA, the Federal Reserve Board, and SEC that identified crosscutting goals, as well as either the internal or external organizations with which the individuals would collaborate to achieve these goals. We have reported that more progress is needed to foster the necessary collaboration both within and across organizational boundaries to achieve results.[5] One strategy for fostering collaboration is identifying in individual performance plans specific programmatic crosscutting goals that would require collaboration to achieve. Another strategy for fostering collaboration is identifying the relevant internal or external organizations with which individuals would collaborate to reinforce a focus across organizational boundaries in individuals' performance plans, as the following examples illustrate.

- At OCC, an employee had an expectation in his individual performance plan to enhance the division's ability to work cooperatively and effectively together with other operational risk divisions, as well as enhance coordination with federal and state agencies and outside banking groups to promote consistency and to advance OCC viewpoints, while contributing to OCC's objective for U.S. and international financial supervisory authorities to cooperate on common interests.
- A senior manager at FCA had a customized expectation in his individual performance plan to work closely with and coordinate Office of Examination initiatives with other offices, notably the Office of General Counsel and Office of Public Affairs, to support the FCA Chairman and Chief Executive Officer's three strategic goals, which are (1) improving communications and relationships with the Farm Credit System, (2) gaining greater efficiency and effectiveness of the agency, and (3) promoting the Farm Credit System to become the Premier Financier of Agriculture and Rural America.
- An executive at the Federal Reserve Board had an expectation in his individual performance plan to undertake expanded discussions with SEC on information-sharing, cooperation, and coordination with the aim of strengthening consolidated supervision and achieving consistency in the implementation of Basel II.[6]
- At SEC, a senior officer in the market regulation division had an expectation in his individual performance plan to advance market regulation objectives through cooperative efforts by coordinating with other SEC offices, other U.S. agencies, self-regulatory organizations, international regulators, and the securities industry.

Agencies Have Included Performance Elements Related to Collaboration or Teamwork in Individual Performance Plans

All of the financial regulators included performance elements related to collaboration or teamwork within and across organizational boundaries in individual performance plans for at least some of their employees. Performance elements related to collaboration or teamwork in individual performance plans can help reinforce behaviors and actions that support crosscutting goals and provide a consistent message to all employees about how they are expected to achieve results. CFTC, FHFB, NCUA, and the Federal Reserve Board provide examples of how standardized performance elements pertaining to teamwork or collaboration have been applied to employees.

- CFTC has established a standardized performance element for all employees that emphasizes collaboration or teamwork, called "Professional Behavior," which requires employees to behave in a professional and cooperative manner when interacting with coworkers or the public and willingly initiate and respond to collaborative efforts with coworkers, among other things.
- At FHFB, all employees have performance elements or standards related to collaboration or teamwork in the standardized performance plans for their occupational groups. For example, the standardized performance plan for executives includes a performance element for "teamwork" that requires executives to collaborate effectively with associates and promote positive and credible relations with associates, among other things. The standardized performance plan for administrative positions also includes a "teamwork" performance element. For the other three occupational groups, collaboration or teamwork is captured in a performance standard. For example, the standardized performance plans for professional positions and managers/supervisors have a performance element that emphasizes collaboration or teamwork, called "Professionalism," which requires the employee to develop and maintain effective working relationships with all employees at all levels throughout the agency and external to the agency and foster effective internal and external communication, among other things.
- NCUA has performance elements related to collaboration or teamwork in the standardized individual performance plans for some occupational groups, such as examiners. For example, in the standardized performance plan for some examiners, there is a performance element for "customer service and teamwork" that requires the individual to demonstrate initiative, responsibility, and accountability to both internal and external customers and work in collaboration with coworkers and others toward common goals.

NCUA officials stated that a collaboration/teamwork performance element may not be applicable to all positions. They also said that, to the extent that this is an appropriate performance element on which an employee should be rated, the agency has or will include it in that employee's performance plan.

- According to Federal Reserve Board officials, the performance plans for some occupations at the agency, such as security and administrative positions, include teamwork as a standard element. Officials also said that customized performance plans for other occupations typically include teamwork or collaboration as a competency.

Agencies Have Used Competencies in Various Ways to Provide a Fuller Assessment of Performance

All 10 of the financial regulatory agencies have used competencies, which define the skills and supporting behaviors that individuals are expected to demonstrate to carry out their work effectively. High-performing organizations use competencies to examine individual contributions to organizational results. We have reported that core competencies applied organizationwide can help reinforce behaviors and actions that support the organization's mission, goals, and values and can provide a consistent message about how employees are expected to achieve results.[7] As previously discussed, while some of the financial regulatory agencies have included customized performance expectations specific to individuals in performance plans, we found that all of the agencies have used competencies. There are some variations in the ways in which the agencies have structured and applied competencies to evaluate employee performance. One of these variations concerns whether or not the agency has assigned different weights to competencies when determining overall summary ratings for individuals.

Agencies Have Applied Competencies Organizationwide

With the exception of the Federal Reserve Board, all of the federal financial regulatory agencies have developed sets of core competencies that apply to groups of employees, and assess employee performance using those competencies as part of the annual performance appraisal process. Using competencies can help strengthen the line of sight between individual performance and organizational success by reinforcing performance expectations that support achievement of the agency's goals, as the following examples illustrate.

- FCA has a different standardized performance plan for each of four occupational groups of employees—senior managers, supervisors, examiners/attorneys/analysts/other specialists (non-supervisory), and administrative/technicians. Each of the plans includes a standard set of competencies, called critical elements, which applies to all employees in that group. Specifically, the performance plan for employees in the examiners/attorneys/analysts/other specialists group contains the following competencies—technical and analytical skills; organizational and project management skills; teamwork and interpersonal skills; written and oral communication skills; and equal employment opportunity (EEO), diversity and other agency initiatives. A few sentences are included on the performance plan form to describe what each element measures in terms of the employee's knowledge, skills, and behavior, as shown in figure 6.
- For the July 2005 to June 2006 performance appraisal cycle we reviewed at CFTC, all employees were assessed on a set of five competencies, called critical elements. Managerial employees were also assessed on three additional competencies having to do with leadership, developing staff, and supporting diversity and EEO programs.
- FDIC has 27 different performance plans with corresponding sets of competencies, called performance criteria, to cover all employees. According to agency officials, FDIC has learned from experience that having a performance management system that is based on standardized sets of competencies has allowed employees' performance to be compared more easily to the standards from period to period. In addition, FDIC's system bases merit pay increases for individuals at least partly on corporate contributions (defined as contributions to corporate, division, or unit-level goals). Officials said that this type of system really enhances employee line of sight and has helped employees focus on how their contributions align with the achievement of organizational goals. In their view, this type of system promotes alignment and consistency more effectively than a system of individual contracts between supervisors and their employees.
- NCUA has approximately 240 detailed performance plans that are tailored to specific occupations and grade levels of employees and that include competencies, which are called elements. All of the employees to whom a particular performance plan applies are assessed on the same set of elements and performance standards. Elements for some employees within the same occupation are universal, but standards can differ by grade level. For example, the performance plans for examiners in grades 7, 11, and 12 all include basically the same elements, but some of the performance standards upon which individuals are to be appraised for each element vary by grade level.

- The Federal Reserve Board differs from the other financial regulatory agencies in the way it uses competencies. The agency does not have sets of core competencies that apply to specified groups of employees across the agency. Instead, divisions have latitude to vary the design and implementation of the performance plan form and process. According to agency officials, divisions select competencies that best suit occupational types and the divisions' goals, because the Board has multiple responsibilities dealing with monetary policy and financial institution regulation. It is possible for employees in the same occupational group, but in different divisions, to be rated against different sets of competencies. Agency officials said that they have not heard complaints from similar occupational groups that they may be assessed against different competencies. Further, all officers, managers, and supervisors are rated against the same four management objectives of communications, staff development, effective planning and administration of financial resources, and equal employment opportunity.

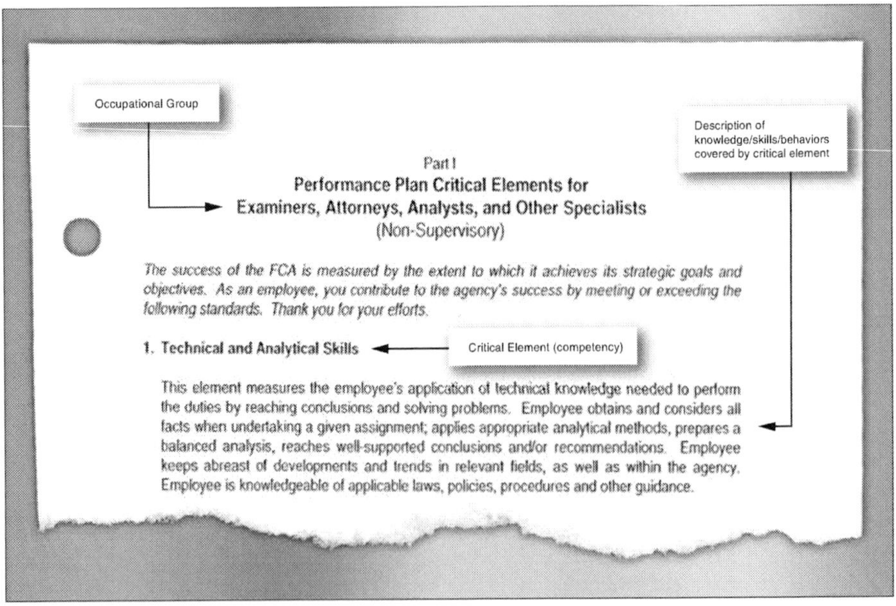

Source: GAO analysis of FCA document.

Figure 6. Excerpt from an FCA Individual Performance Plan.

Agencies Have Assigned Weights to Competencies

A few of the agencies, such as OFHEO, FCA, and NCUA, allow differing weights to be assigned to specific competencies when determining overall summary performance ratings for individuals. Using weights enables the organization to place more emphasis on selected competencies that are deemed to be more important in assessing the overall performance of individuals in particular positions. Other agencies, including OCC, OTS, FDIC, CFTC, and FHFB, do not assign differing weights to competencies, as the following examples illustrate.

- At OFHEO, the rating official for each employee assigns a weight to each of the competencies (called performance elements) included in the individual's performance plan, in consultation with the reviewing official. Each competency must have a minimum weight of at least 5, with the total weight of all the competencies in an individual performance plan equaling 100. Any competency with a weight of 20 or higher is considered to be critical. Each competency element is weighted and scored (see figure 7), and then the weighted ratings for the competencies are summed to derive the total summary rating for the individual.[8]
- FCA also permits supervisors to assign different weights to competencies for individual employees, within the standardized performance plans, at the beginning of the appraisal period. No competency can be weighted less than 5 percent or more than 40 percent.
- At NCUA, the elements for the various occupations and grade levels have different weights assigned to them, depending on the priorities and skills pertaining to the positions. The weights are specified on the performance plan form for each position.
- Some of the financial regulatory agencies, including OCC, OTS, FDIC, CFTC, and FHFB, do not assign different weights to competencies when appraising employee performance. Instead, all of the competencies in an employee's performance plan are equally considered during the appraisal. For example, at OCC, all of the competencies (which are called skill-based performance elements) that are contained in an individual's performance plan are considered to be critical, so they receive equal weight when determining the overall summary rating for that individual, according to an official.

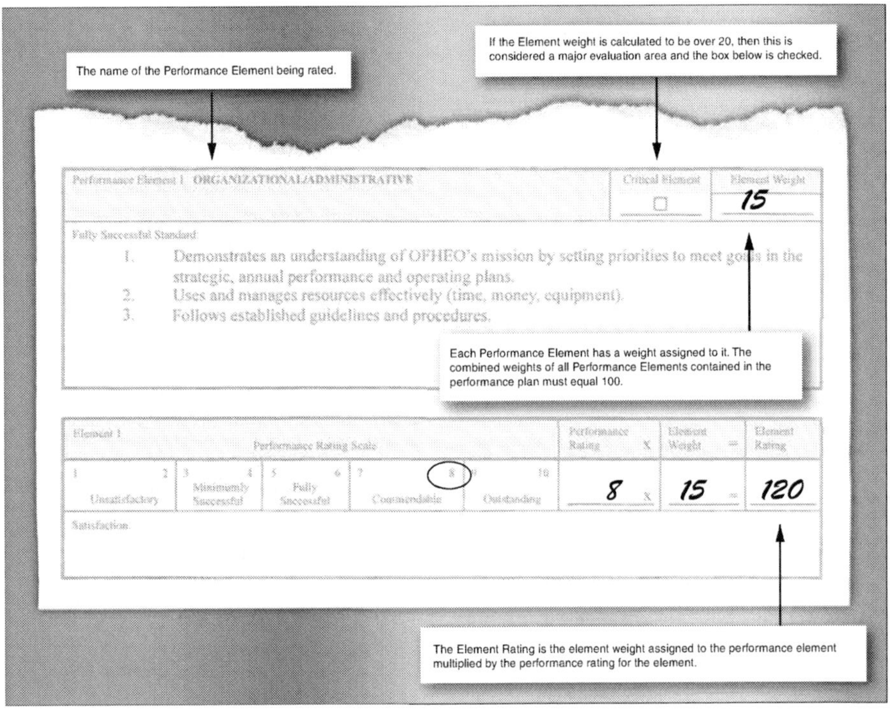

Source: GAO analysis of OFHEO document.

Figure 7. Example of OFHEO's Worksheet for Weighting Performance Elements.

Agencies Have Involved Employees and Stakeholders in Various Ways to Gain Ownership of Performance Management Systems

The financial regulatory agencies have used several strategies to involve employees in their systems, including (1) soliciting or considering input from employees on developing or refining their performance management systems, (2) offering employees opportunities to participate in the performance planning and appraisal process, and (3) ensuring that employees were adequately trained on the performance management system when rolling out the system and when changes were made to the system. Overall, the 10 agencies have employed these strategies differently. Effective performance management systems depend on individuals', their supervisors', and management's common understanding, support, and use of these systems to reinforce the connection between performance management and organizational results. Employee involvement improves the quality of the system by providing a front-line perspective and helping to create organizationwide understanding and ownership.

Agencies Have Considered Employee Input for Developing or Refining Performance Management Systems

All of the financial regulatory agencies, in some way, solicited or considered employee input for developing or refining their performance management systems by working with unions or employee groups to gather employee opinions or conducting employee surveys or focus groups. An important step to ensure the success of a new performance management system is to consult a wide range of stakeholders and to do so early in the process. High-performing organizations have found that actively involving employees and stakeholders, such as unions or other employee groups that represent employee views, when developing results-oriented performance management systems helps to improve employees' confidence and belief in the fairness of the system and increase their understanding and ownership of organizational goals and objectives. Feedback obtained from these sources is also important when creating or refining competencies and performance standards used in performance plans. However, in order for employees to gain ownership of the system, employee input must receive adequate acknowledgement and consideration from management.

Agencies Have Involved Employee Groups in the Performance Management System Process

Unions and employee groups had some role in providing comments or input into the performance management systems at some of the financial regulators. Six of the regulators (CFTC, FDIC, NCUA, OCC, OTS, and SEC) had active union chapters, and four agencies (FCA, Federal Reserve Board, FHFB, and OFHEO) had employee groups.[9] We have previously reported that obtaining union cooperation and support through effective labor-management relations can help achieve consensus on planned changes to a system, avoid misunderstandings, and more expeditiously resolve problems that occur.[10] The degree to which unions and employee groups were involved in providing comments or input into the development or implementation of performance management systems varied from agency to agency. A few of the agencies with unions have to negotiate over compensation. Unions at some agencies were involved in participating in negotiations, entering into formal agreements such as contracts and memoranda of understanding, and initiating litigation concerning the development or implementation of performance management systems. At other regulators, employee groups were invited to comment on aspects of the performance management system, as the following examples illustrate.

- OFHEO has used ad hoc employee working groups to study different human capital issues and advise management on recommendations for changes. Specifically, OFHEO established a working group to look at teamwork and communication in the agency and the group recommended changes to the individual performance plans relevant to teamwork and communications. As a result of the group's recommendation, OFHEO included additional language for the agency's performance plans in the performance elements of teamwork and communication.
- At FDIC, the union participated with management in formal negotiations regarding the establishment of the agency's performance management and pay for performance systems and how the systems would work. Both parties are bound by the terms of the formal agreements that resulted.
- At NCUA, union representatives together with management issued a memorandum of understanding in June 2006 detailing how supervisors are supposed to introduce new performance plans for specified examiner positions. The agreement set the timing of the introduction of new performance standards, required training for rating officials, required supervisors to give progress reviews to their employees on achievements to date, and required supervisors and employees to discuss the new standards.
- SEC will implement a new compensation and benefits system as a result of an October 2006 ruling from the Federal Service Impasses Panel (Panel).[11] The Panel became involved when SEC and union negotiations over a compensation and benefits agreement reached an impasse. SEC management told us that they have formed a labor-management working committee to discuss how to implement the terms of the new Compensation and Benefits Agreement as provided for under the Panel ruling.

Agencies Have Directly Engaged Employees in Consultations about the Performance Management System

The financial regulatory agencies involved employees in different ways when developing their performance management systems. This process can involve directly engaging individual employees and collecting opinions from all employees through focus groups, surveys, or other forms of feedback to develop a successful performance management system. Further, soliciting employee input is also important when developing or revising competencies or performance elements and related performance standards in a performance management system in order to ensure that the competencies and standards reflect skills and behaviors that are relevant to employee tasks and responsibilities. While all of the financial regulators involved employees to some degree, as the following examples illustrate, NCUA did not consistently solicit input on developing or revising the competencies and standards.

- In 2003-2004, when the Federal Reserve Board sought to revamp its performance management system, the agency hired an outside consultant to conduct focus groups with the intent of identifying issues raised by employees and making recommendations to address any concerns. Some focus group participants said that the agency's recommended rating distribution guidelines might prevent some employees from achieving a rating in the highest category. Furthermore, some employees were concerned about possible unfairness in ratings and wanted to see the distribution of the performance ratings for all employees published. As a result of this feedback, management began publishing the agency's ratings distributions, and added information on the system's process to the agency's internal Web site on the performance management system.
- When developing its first performance-based pay system in 2006, CFTC solicited employee input through a variety of methods. The agency hired a contractor to conduct focus groups and to survey employees about transitioning to a performance-based pay system and the administration of a performance management system. The contractor also hosted a Webinar, a Web-based interactive seminar that allows for the submission of anonymous questions and comments, to present the results of the employee survey. Additionally, CFTC conducted town hall meetings to inform employees about development of the system. As a result of employee feedback, management decided to delay the first phase of implementation of the system from July 2006 until October 2006 in order to allow additional time for employees to learn about the system and make the transition. Union representatives at CFTC (Chicago and New York) told us that prior to CFTC's transition to performance-based pay, the agency's management communicated frequently with the union and provided appropriate notice prior to implementing changes.
- Through internal surveys, OFHEO received feedback on employee concerns regarding opportunities for promotion and the frequency of progress reviews. According to an agency official, feedback from an employee survey indicated that employees wanted more opportunities for promotion than the prior six pay-band system allowed. On the basis of this employee feedback, OFHEO made the decision to switch to 18 pay grades and created career ladders. Further, employees commented through the survey that they wanted more feedback on their performance during the year. As a result, OFHEO

increased the number of progress review meetings from two to four per year. An agency official stated that the Office of Human Resources Management monitors these meetings to ensure that they have been held.

- SEC has analyzed data on SEC responses to OPM's governmentwide Federal Human Capital Survey. According to agency officials, SEC has tracked employee responses to questions on, for example, how well the agency rewards good performers and deals with poor performers. In addition, SEC has created a mailbox for anonymous employee comments and constructive criticism on the performance management system.
- FCA circulated a draft of its proposed performance management system in 2002, and solicited comments from employees. As a result of employee comments, FCA revised the descriptions of performance elements in the performance plans, changed the weight of an element dealing with equal opportunity employment, eliminated one element, and provided additional guidance and training. To show how employee feedback was addressed, FCA management presented a briefing to employees, which listed some of the employee comments about the individual performance plans with accompanying responses from management.
- According to an NCUA official present at the time when the agency originally developed its performance elements and standards, NCUA conducted job analysis studies for all positions, which involved employees and supervisors in identifying specific duties, skills, and competencies needed to accomplish different jobs. In addition to the studies, she said that NCUA surveyed employees and conducted an assessment to identify any gaps in the performance elements and standards. In 2006, when NCUA revised the elements and standards for some examiner positions, NCUA used a committee consisting of managers, supervisors, and one employee to develop the new elements and standards. Union representatives told us they were briefed on the final version of the elements and standards, but were not asked for input. NCUA is currently revising individual performance plans for other positions and the process does not include provisions for soliciting and incorporating employee input. In comments on the draft of this report, NCUA officials stated that NCUA sought to solicit input from employees for certain positions, but that it was not necessary for positions that are common across the government, since NCUA usually adopts the competencies established by OPM for those positions.

Some union and employee group representatives we spoke with did not think that management gave adequate consideration to employee input. For example, the Employees' Committee at the Federal Reserve Board, which provides advice to the Management Division on a variety of issues, was asked to provide comments during the latest revision of the performance management system. According to committee members, the committee submitted a paper containing recommendations in response to this management request. The committee, however, did not receive a written response from management acknowledging their recommended changes. Committee members told us they are now hesitant to submit input during the current strategic planning process because they are concerned about the usefulness of putting time and energy into developing recommendations that may not be considered. According to agency officials, the responses from the Employees' Committee and other employee focus groups held on this topic were summarized by the consultant hired for the project and the consultant presented the summary comments to management through the executive oversight committee. In addition, management officials stated that they met with other committee members (i.e., the heads of special interest groups) to discuss their input. The Federal Reserve Board's Administrative Governor has also held monthly meetings with randomly selected employees as an opportunity for employees to voice their concerns about the performance management program, among other topics.

Agencies Have Encouraged Employee Participation in Performance Planning and Appraisals

All of the agencies, including FCA and FHFB, required or encouraged employee participation in developing individual performance plans or writing self assessments, contribution statements, or reports summarizing accomplishments at the end of the appraisal cycle. In high-performing organizations, employees and supervisors share the responsibility for individual performance management and both should be actively involved in identifying how individuals can contribute to organizational results and be held accountable for their contributions. By actively participating, employees are not just recipients of performance expectations and ratings, but rather, have their ideas heard and considered in work planning and assessment decisions. However, employee representatives from some agencies, such as FDIC, OTS, and OCC, expressed concern that employees were not actively involved in the performance planning and appraisal processes even when the agency required or encouraged such participation.[12]

- At FCA, employees could participate in performance planning by working with their rating officials to identify accomplishments expected to be achieved during the appraisal period. In addition to participating in an official mid-year performance review, at the end of the appraisal cycle, employees and supervisors could meet for a pre-appraisal interview to discuss the employees' accomplishments during the previous year. Additionally, employees could submit an optional self assessment of their performance. This input was supposed to be considered when the supervisor evaluated the employee, according to FCA policy.

- Employees at FHFB had several options for participating in developing their performance plans—working with the supervisor to develop the plan, providing the supervisor with a draft plan, or commenting on a plan prepared by the supervisor.

Although FDIC, OTS, and OCC provided some opportunities for employee participation in the planning and appraisal processes, we heard from union representatives at these agencies that this participation did not always occur, as the following examples illustrate.

- FDIC's performance management directive requires that the employee and the supervisor have a meeting to discuss all performance criteria included in the employee's performance plan and any expectations regarding the quality, quantity or timeliness of work assignments. The policy also encourages the employee to submit an accomplishment report and to submit written comments on his or her supervisor's draft assessment of the employee's "Total Performance" before it is forwarded to higher levels of review within a pay pool. However, union representatives told us that expectation-setting meetings have not been consistently conducted; instead, sometimes employees have simply signed a form to acknowledge receipt of their performance plans. Additionally, employee comments on the appraisal form have not been taken into account by supervisors, according to union representatives. FDIC officials stated that the rating official and employee are required to meet to discuss expectations at the beginning of the rating period or whenever there is a change in performance criteria. Officials also noted that the performance management program is a collaborative process that relies on communication between a manager and his or her employees, and that the employee is supposed to seek clarification on performance criteria or expectations from the supervisor if necessary, as is explained in the directive.
- An employee union representative at OTS maintained that employees have not been very involved in setting their own performance expectations; instead, supervisors have informed them about what they should do at the beginning of the performance appraisal cycle. The representative told us that supervisors may discuss changing expectations with employees during the year, but these discussions have not always occurred. According to an agency official, OTS has encouraged managers to regularly meet with their employees and provide a clear picture of what is expected of employees for the year in terms of their individual roles and responsibilities for the

standardized performance expectations and what will be considered in appraising the employees' performance.

- Although OCC provided opportunities for employee participation in the performance planning and appraisal processes, union representatives told us that this participation did not always occur. At OCC, employees may participate in developing their individual performance plans and are supposed to submit accomplishment reports. Further, officials explained that many employees at OCC have secondary objectives in their performance plans. Because secondary objectives are customized, there should be a discussion between the supervisor and the employee. According to an official, if an employee has customized secondary objectives included in his or her individual performance plan, the employee and supervisor are supposed to have a discussion about it.[13] However, representatives from the union at OCC told us that performance plans are pretty generic and are distributed to individuals based on their grade levels. They said that some employees do not sit with their managers to tailor the plans; instead, employees just sign the forms to acknowledge receipt of the plans.

Agencies Have Provided Training on Performance Management Systems

All of the financial regulatory agencies have conducted some form of training or information dissemination on topics related to performance management. Asking employees to provide feedback should not be a onetime process, but an ongoing process that occurs through the training of employees at all levels of the organization to ensure common understanding of the evaluation, implementation, and results of the systems. Providing training when changes are made to a performance management system can help ensure that employees stay connected to the system and reinforce the importance of connecting individual performance expectations to organizational goals. At some agencies, such as SEC and FHFB, training has been mainly directed at supervisors, while at FDIC training has been given to non-managers as well. Formal training for non-supervisors at the agencies has typically been directed at new employees or has occurred when significant changes were being made to a performance management system. Some agencies have distributed materials through the agency intranet, memos, emails, or other written documents, as the following examples illustrate.

- SEC has offered several opportunities for supervisors to learn the mechanics and skills necessary for administering the performance management system. Specifically, new supervisors have received general training on supervisory roles and responsibilities, including performance management. For supervisors, SEC has offered two levels of classes on managing performance and communicating expectations. Supervisors have also had the opportunity to receive training on managing labor relations, which has included discussions of SEC's agreement with the union, and the performance-based pay and award systems. Supervisors could also attend a briefing on performance management concepts and processes. In addition to offering supervisor training, SEC informs new employees about the performance management system during the orientation program. Performance management information is also available to employees through the agency's intranet web site. Finally, supervisors are supposed to brief new employees on the performance management system at the beginning of the rating cycle, during discussions of individual performance standards.

- Most employees at FHFB have not received training on performance management since the late 1990s, and are expected to learn about the system from their supervisors. However, FHFB offered training for managers and supervisors in 2004 on the performance management system and how to conduct performance appraisals.
- FDIC has conducted several training sessions and disseminated information to managers and employees related to its performance management and pay for performance programs. This has included in-person training sessions, taped sessions made available for viewing on IPTV, and "question and answer" documents and policy directives available on the agency intranet. FDIC provided specific training for nonsupervisors in 2006 when management and union representatives jointly conducted training sessions on the agency's new compensation agreement. Training was intended for non-management employees, including bargaining unit and non-bargaining unit employees, and was conducted in a variety of formats. Sessions included discussions of employees' roles and responsibilities in the performance management and pay for performance systems.

Agencies Generally Have Linked Pay to Performance and Built-in Safeguards

As discussed, the 10 financial regulatory agencies linked pay to performance and built safeguards into their performance management systems but could make improvements to ensure that poor performers do not receive pay increases and to improve the communication of performance standards and transparency of performance results. This section provides more detailed information on the different ways in which the agencies translated performance ratings into pay increases and used different budgeting strategies for performance-based pay. The section also discusses how the agencies awarded pay increases that considered performance but were not dependent on ratings. Finally, information is presented on agency implementation of two additional safeguards: higher-level reviews of performance rating decisions and establishing appeals processes for performance rating decisions.

Agencies Used Differing Methods to Translate Performance Ratings into Pay Increases

For increases that were linked to performance ratings, the financial regulatory agencies used different methods to translate employee performance ratings into pay increases. These methods included establishing ranges for increases, using formulas, and considering current salaries when making decisions on the amounts of performance-based pay increases for individuals.

Several agencies established ranges of potential pay increases corresponding to the various performance rating levels. These systems gave managers the discretion to determine the exact pay increase amounts for individuals, within those ranges, as the following examples illustrate.

- At OTS, employees who received a rating of 5 (on a 5-level scale) received between a 5.5 percent and 7.5 percent pay increase, while employees who received a rating of 3 received between a 1.5 percent and 3.25 percent pay increase during the appraisal cycle we reviewed. Employees who received a rating of 1 or 2 did not receive any pay increase. OTS gave managers the flexibility to determine the specific pay amount each employee would receive within the range of possible pay increases corresponding to that performance rating.
- OCC established ranges of potential pay increases that corresponded to different performance rating levels and gave managers the flexibility to decide on the exact amount of pay increase that each individual would receive within the range that corresponded to that employee's rating level. Each year OCC adopts a merit pay matrix that defines a range of allowable percentage increases that may be paid for performance rating levels 3 and 4 (the two highest rating categories). During the appraisal cycle we reviewed, individuals with a level 3 performance rating were eligible to receive a merit increase between 2.1 percent and 5.5 percent, and individuals with a level 4 rating could receive a merit increase between 5 percent and 9 percent. The rating official recommended the percentage of merit pay that each employee with a summary rating of 3 or 4 should receive. Agency officials told us that

it can be challenging for managers to determine the pay increase amount for each employee within those pre-stablished pay increase ranges. Managers want to ensure consistency among employees with similar levels of performance and often consult with other managers or human resources staff for advice when making these pay increase decisions. Employee representatives expressed some concern about the overlapping ranges for pay increases, and a representative said that employees are unclear about what performance behaviors are needed to achieve merit increases.

Other agencies used formulas for determining the amounts of pay increases linked to performance ratings to be awarded, as the following example illustrates.

- NCUA used a pay matrix tied to employees' performance rating scores (which could range from 0 to 300) to calculate the pay increase percentages. All employees in the same pay pool that received the same performance rating would receive the same pay increase percentage. Specifically, an employee who received a performance rating score of 234 fell within the "fully successful" performance rating range and received a pay increase of 3.066 percent. Another employee who received a performance rating score of 235 fell within the "highly successful" performance rating range and received a pay increase of 3.076 percent. Employees who received a performance rating score below 165 fell within the "unsatisfactory" or "minimally successful" performance rating ranges and did not receive any pay increases.

Some agencies considered employees' current salaries when deciding on the amounts for pay increases linked to performance ratings, as the following example illustrates.

- At FCA, the percentage pay increase an employee received depended on where the employee's current salary fell within the pay band. FCA used a merit matrix to calculate merit pay increases. The matrix considered an employee's existing salary position within the relevant pay band (with position defined in terms of one of five possible quintiles), as well as the employee's performance rating, and determined the percentage pay increase corresponding to those factors. For example, for the performance appraisal cycle we reviewed at FCA, the percentage increase in pay that an employee who received a fully successful performance rating could receive ranged from 3.5 percent (for an individual whose salary was in the bottom quintile of the pay band) to 2.0 percent (for an individual whose salary was in the top quintile of the pay band). For employees with the same performance rating, an employee whose salary was considered to be below market rate at the bottom of the pay band would receive a larger percentage pay increase than an employee whose salary was considered to be at or above market rate. FCA provided pay increases only to employees who performed above a minimally successful rating level.

At many of the agencies, as an employee's salary approached the top of the pay range for a position, increases linked to performance ratings could be received as a combination of permanent salary increase and a one-time, lump sum cash payment, as the following example illustrates.

- At FHFB, for an employee in a position with a pay range of $70,000–$90,000, if the individual's salary was near the top of the pay range, he or she would receive a performance-based merit increase to take his or her salary to the top of the salary range and then receive a lump sum payment.

Across the various methods used to translate performance ratings into pay increases, the expectation would be that larger pay increases are associated with higher performance ratings. As a means of providing a quantified descriptor of how strongly increases in ratings were associated with increases in pay linked to those ratings at each of the agencies, we computed a Spearman rank correlation coefficient between employees' performance ratings and the percentage increases in pay that were linked to performance ratings.[14] Although the correlation coefficients for the eight agencies varied from +0.63 and +0.94, they all demonstrated a strong positive association between higher performance ratings and higher ratings-linked pay increases (expressed as a percentage increase in salary).[15]

While the correlation coefficients provide some additional perspective on the linkage between performance ratings and pay increases at the financial regulatory agencies, they should be viewed as a rough gauge of the overall strength of the relationship across the agencies and are not sufficient for ranking or making other comparisons between agencies.[16] In reviewing the coefficients, we noted that agencies with some of the lowest correlations were using a four-level rating system that produced rather constrained ratings distributions. In one instance, for example, employees rated at the two lowest performance levels (called levels 1 and 2) were not eligible for pay increases, and over two-thirds of all employees received a level 3 rating. Both the base pay increases and bonus amounts that could be awarded for level 3 performance overlapped with those for level 4 (the highest level), such that some employees rated at level 3 realized a percentage increase in pay that was twice the amount obtained by other level-3-rated employees, as well as even some level-4-rated employees.

Agencies Used Different Budgeting Strategies for Performance-Based Pay

The federal financial agencies also varied in their strategies to budget for pay increases directly linked to performance ratings. Many of the agencies set aside funds each year for performance-based pay increases. At some agencies, these funds were treated as an agencywide funding pool or pools for performance-based pay increases, as the following examples illustrate.

- According to agency officials, NCUA established two agencywide merit funding pools for different employee grade-level groups because higher graded employees usually received higher ratings and consequently, higher merit pay increases. Officials stated that the establishment of two merit funding pools was more advantageous to lower graded employees and increased the amount of funds available for their merit pay.
- SEC established one pool of funds for performance bonuses and quality step increases available for senior officers, and another pool for all other employees.

At some agencies the performance-based pay increases budget was divided into separate pay pools by suborganizational unit, and the responsibility for distributing merit pay increases was delegated to management at the subunit level, as the following examples illustrate.[17]

- For the "Pay for Performance" program at FDIC that covers bargaining unit and non-bargaining unit employees, the agency established pay pools at the division level (and at the regional level for the large Division of Supervision and Consumer Protection), and allocated funds for performance-based pay increases to the pools. Funds were allocated through pay pools to each division and office, with subsequent separations of each division or office into separate populations for bargaining unit and non-bargaining unit employees. (Corporate managers and executives at FDIC are covered by a separate pay-at-risk compensation system.)
- FHFB provided each office with a pay pool for performance-based annual pay increases. The merit increase pool amounts were determined based on the approved governmentwide general increase plus 2.5 percent of the total base salaries for all employees in the office. An FHFB official stated that the reason each office was provided with a pool of funds was to avoid comparing individuals with different functions and responsibilities to each other, and this official believed that FHFB had greater control when pay decisions were

made at the office level. For example, an office director could decide to assess all his staff at the outstanding level, but less performance-based pay would be available for each office employee. Office directors were responsible for determining the sum of all merit increases and lump sum payments for their offices, while not exceeding their offices' merit increase pool allocations.

Agencies Provided Other Increases That Considered Performance

In addition to providing ratings-based pay increases, the financial regulatory agencies awarded pay increases that considered individual performance in some way without being directly linked to employees' performance ratings. The following are additional examples of these types of pay increases at the agencies to supplement the material presented in the body of the report.

- The Federal Reserve Board offered a cash awards program, which accounted for about 2.5 percent of the total agency salary budget, to reward employees who sustained exceptional performance or made significant contributions to successful projects, according to officials. According to the Federal Reserve Board's criteria for this awards program, cash awards could be given to employees who initiated, recommended, or accomplished actions that achieved important Federal Reserve Board goals, realized significant cost reductions, or improved the productivity or quality of Board services. These awards could be made in any amount up to a maximum of 10 percent of an employee's base pay within the same performance cycle. The 10 percent maximum did not apply to variable pay awards, which are given instead of cash awards to economists, attorneys, or Federal Reserve Board officers.
- For some regulators, these types of pay increases were sizeable. For example, at OCC, approximately 10 percent of employees were awarded a special increase during the completed appraisal cycle we reviewed. The awards represented a 5 percent raise for those individuals. According to OCC policy, special increases are to be awarded to recognize increased value an employee contributes to his or her job by applying desirable skills over a significant period of time or by assuming higher-level responsibilities within his or her pay band. OCC also provided some pay increases for competitive and noncompetitive promotions during the appraisal cycle we reviewed. Interestingly, of the eight financial regulators that participated in OPM's 2006 Federal Human Capital Survey, OCC had the largest percentage of employees agreeing with the view that awards in their work units depended on how well employees performed their jobs. At OCC, 55.7 percent of

employees agreed with this view. Governmentwide the corresponding figure was 39.8 percent of employees. Two other agencies, FCA and NCUA, also had slightly over 50 percent of their employees agreeing with this statement.

Results from the 2006 OPM Federal Human Capital Survey suggest that the financial regulatory agencies have done relatively better than many agencies governmentwide in linking pay to performance. All eight of the financial regulators that participated in the 2006 survey had percentages of positive responses from their employees that were about the same as or better than the governmentwide percentage of 21.7 positive responses to an item asking employees whether they agreed or disagreed with the statement that pay raises depended on how well employees performed their jobs at their agencies. The percentage of employees giving a positive response to this item was at least twice as high as the governmentwide value for a majority of the eight agencies participating in the survey.

Agencies Built in Safeguards

While the financial regulatory agencies built safeguards into their performance management systems, the agencies established and communicated standards for differentiating among performance rating categories and criteria for performance-based pay decisions to varying degrees. The agencies also built in additional safeguards of establishing higher-level reviews of performance rating decisions by either higher-level officials or oversight groups, and all have established appeals processes for employees to request reconsiderations of performance rating decisions. It is important for agencies to have modern, effective, credible, and, as appropriate, validated performance management systems in place with adequate safeguards to ensure fairness and prevent politicization and abuse. We have reported that a common concern that employees express about any performance-based pay system is whether supervisors have the ability and willingness to assess employees' performance fairly.[18] Using safeguards can help to allay these concerns and build a fair and credible system.

Agencies Implemented Higher-Level Reviews of Performance Rating Decisions

Although they have used different approaches, all of the federal financial regulatory agencies have provided higher-level reviews of individual performance rating decisions to help ensure that performance standards were consistently and equitably applied across the agency. All of the agencies have established at least one level of review of employees' performance ratings to help ensure that performance standards were applied appropriately. At some agencies, this oversight process has involved a second-line supervisor or higher-level official reviewing the employee's performance rating to ensure that the rating was appropriate and consistent with any narrative describing the employee's performance. Some agencies also have offices outside of the employee's team/office, such as the Human Capital Office, review employee performance ratings to ensure that rating decisions for groups of employees (agencywide, or by division or region) were fair and equitable, as the following examples illustrate.

- OCC officials indicated that at the end of every appraisal cycle, they have evaluated the results of the performance management and pay system by looking, for example, at the differentiation in ratings and pay decisions and how the pay ranges were used. The human resources officials have discussed these results with managers to show them how their employees' performance ratings and pay decisions influenced OCC's overall results. For example, OCC introduced merit bonuses for the first time in the 2005 performance appraisal cycle. Upon reviewing the results of the merit bonus decisions, OCC officials found that the percentage of employees in each organizational unit that received a merit bonus varied widely among the units—ranging from a high of over 80 percent of employees receiving a bonus in one unit to 30 percent in another unit. As a result, according to agency officials, OCC decided to recommend a minimum amount for bonuses and restrict the percentage of staff who can receive a bonus to 50 percent within each organizational unit. Agency officials also indicated that they have identified areas of future training on the system based on the results of reviews and subsequent discussions with managers, in order to improve implementation of the system.
- At NCUA, an employee's performance rating was completed and signed by the rating official, and then a reviewing official (an office or regional director) reviewed the employee's performance rating to ensure that the rating was supported. Reviewers also look for consistency throughout the rating process. For example, an Associate Regional Director will look across all examiners' ratings in the region for consistency.
- FHFB provided a supervisory review of performance ratings to help ensure that an employee's recommended rating was justified as well as consistent with other ratings in the employee's work group. Once the rating official (usually a first-line supervisor) recommended an initial summary rating, the rating official would forward the rating to a second-line supervisory reviewer (usually the division director or deputy director), called a reviewing official. According to FHFB officials, the reviewing official was usually knowledgeable about the employee's performance and could discuss the

rating narrative and final rating decision with the rating official before the rating was shared with the employee. In addition, the reviewing official checked whether performance rating narratives supported individual performance elements, summary ratings were properly calculated and appropriately signed, and there was consistency of ratings across the work group. FHFB employee representatives with whom we spoke stated a belief that the rating review process was effective and that supervisors did not give ratings unless they first reviewed their decisions with management. Employee representatives noted that there is a commitment in the agency to be fair and equitable in assigning ratings.

- FCA provided multiple levels of reviews of ratings to ensure the appropriateness of rating scores and consistency in applying performance standards across FCA offices. After the rating official completed an initial rating, a second-line reviewer was assigned to review each employee's rating against the standards. Before final ratings were issued, FCA's Office of Management Services provided a check to ensure that offices were appropriately and consistently applying performance standards and to look for any significant outliers. Employee performance assessments rated as outstanding and as less than fully successful would be reviewed to determine whether rating scores matched the narrative discussions. Any potential issues identified would be brought to the attention of the rating official for discussion and resolution. Management officials told us that the Chief Human Capital Officer would meet with division management to discuss whether the rating criteria were appropriately applied and then division managers would determine whether to change any performance ratings. In addition, the Office of Management Services performed a post-rating distribution audit to review final rating distributions to help inform future rating practices.

Establish Appeals Processes for Performance Rating Decisions

As mentioned previously, all of the federal financial regulatory agencies have established appeals processes for employees to request reconsiderations of performance rating decisions to help ensure accuracy and fairness in the process. Providing mechanisms for employees to dispute rating decisions when they believe decisions are unfair can help employees gain more trust in the system, as the following examples illustrate.

- Employees at CFTC could ask for an appeal of their overall rating through the agency's reconsideration process. An employee could first appeal his or her rating to the manager who reviewed the rating (called the reviewing official) by defending his or her position orally or in writing. This Reviewing Official then considered the employee's justification as well as the original rater's opinion and provided a final decision on the matter. According to CFTC officials, employees sometimes wanted to change the wording in their performance evaluations.

- OTS has defined a grievance policy for employees who are dissatisfied with their performance ratings. Employees covered by the bargaining unit agreement may file a grievance under the negotiated agreement while employees not covered by the agreement may request a grievance (within 10 days of receiving their ratings) under the agency's administrative grievance procedures. OTS' union representative reported that in the past, management and union representatives had resolved many cases of rating disputes prior to employees filing formal grievances.
- The Federal Reserve Board has established an appeals process so that an employee can appeal the fairness of an overall rating decision, the rating on an individual element, or any adverse comments appearing on the performance assessment form. Employee representatives we spoke with said that they believe that employees understand the appeals process, but thought that more employees could take advantage of this opportunity. An employee may first appeal his or her performance rating to a division director, who in turn will notify the appropriate supervisor who submitted the rating. Then, the division director will determine whether the rating is appropriate based upon a review of documentation provided by both the employee and supervisor. If the employee is not satisfied with the first-level appeal decision, the employee may make a second-level appeal to the Associate Director of Human Resources and specify areas of disagreement with the performance assessment. The Associate Director for the second-level appeal will then determine whether the division has reasonably followed procedures and whether performance assessment guidelines were applied consistently to other employees reporting to the same supervisor. This supporting documentation submitted by the division will be shared with the employee, except in cases where doing so infringes on the confidentiality of other employees. As a result, first- or second- level appeal decisions may result in changes to an overall rating, changes to the rating of an individual element, or changes in the language in the employee's performance assessment.
- OFHEO has established a three-level appeals process to ensure that employees can dispute rating decisions when they disagree with rating decisions. Employees can appeal the overall performance rating or individual performance elements within the rating. For the first-level appeal, the employee can submit a request with supporting documentation to the performance rating official for reconsideration. If an appeal is not resolved at

the first level, the employee can request that the second-level supervisor review the performance rating and supporting documentation. Finally, the employee can request a third-level appeal by the third-level supervisor, if necessary.

Appendix IV. Actions Taken by Financial Regulators to Seek to Maintain Pay and Benefits Comparability and Pay and Benefits Data

The federal financial regulatory agencies have made an effort to meet the comparability requirements as required by the Financial Institutions Reform, Recovery, and Enforcement Act of 1989 (FIRREA) and subsequent legislation.[1] However, we found that factors such as funding constraints, when the agency was granted flexibility under Title V of the U.S. Code, the needs or preferences of their respective workforces, and each agency's pay and benefits policies can result in some variation in their pay and benefits.[2] They have also taken steps to explore a common survey that would enable them to more efficiently collect information for pay and benefit comparability purposes.

Financial Regulators Have Conducted Individual Pay and Benefits Comparability Surveys and Regularly Consult with Each Other, but Noted Some Inefficiencies in the Process

To seek to maintain pay and benefits comparability, the majority of the 10 federal financial regulators have hired external compensation consultants to conduct individual formal pay and benefits comparability surveys that have included the other financial regulators. As shown in table 5, 7 of the 10 financial regulators conducted pay and benefits comparability surveys. Of the 7, 5 agencies also have included benefits in their formal surveys. According to agency officials, because some of the 10 agencies perceive the private sector as their main competitor for skilled employees, they have included private-sector entities in their pay and benefits surveys or have obtained additional private-sector data through the Bureau of Labor Statistics and private vendors to complement their pay and benefits surveys.

Table 5. Pay and Benefits Surveys That Federal Financial Regulators Conducted through External Compensation Consultants, 1991-2006

Agencies	Hired external compensation consultants to conduct pay comparability surveys	Included benefits in compara-bility surveys	Years in which agencies have conducted surveys through external compensation consultants	Agencies participating in surveys
CFTC	No. In 2003 and 2005, used consultant to review existing surveys.	N/A	N/A	Used FDIC and OCC 2002 survey results in 2003; used interagency group data in 2005.
FCA	Conducts a pay survey once every 2–3 years.	No	1991, 1993, 1996, 1999, 2002	The 2002 survey included FDIC, FHFB, the Federal Reserve Board, NCUA, OCC, OFHEO, and OTS.
FDIC	Conducts pay and benefits survey about once every 3 years.	Yes	1996, 1999, 2002, 2005	The 2005 pay survey included all FIRREA agencies as well as the Federal Reserve Board, CFTC, OFHEO, SEC, and several Federal Reserve Banks. The 2005 benefits survey included all FIRREA agencies and the Federal Reserve Board.
FHFB	Conducted a pay and benefits survey once. Also uses FDIC's pay and benefits surveys as a guide.	Yes	2002	The 2003 survey compared pay and benefits with FCA, FDIC, OCC, NCUA, OTS, and the Federal Reserve Board.

Table 5. (Continued)

Agencies	Hired external compensation consultants to conduct pay comparability surveys	Included benefits in compara-bility surveys	Years in which agencies have conducted surveys through external compensation consultants	Agencies participating in surveys
Federal Reserve Board	Conducts pay and benefits survey every 1–2 years.	Yes	Annual surveys conducted between 1994 and 2005, excluding 2003.	The 2005 survey included OCC, FDIC, NCUA, OFHEO, OTS, SEC, as well as the private-sector entities and academia.
NCUA	Conducted pay and benefits surveys twice.	Yes	2000, 2004	The 2004 pay and benefits survey included FDIC, OCC, OTS, FHFB, FCA, SEC, OFHEO, and the private sector.
OCC	Conducted a pay survey every year, alternating between a full survey that covered many benchmarked jobs and a simplified survey that covered a few of the benchmarked jobs.	No	1999, 2001, 2002, 2003, 2006	The 2006 pay survey included FCA, FDIC, FHFB, NCUA, OTS, OFHEO, SEC, and the Federal Reserve Board.
OFHEO	Conducted pay and benefits surveys every 3 to 5 years.	Yes	2000, 2005	The 2005 pay and benefits survey included OCC, the Federal Reserve Board, FDIC, OTS, FHFB, and FCA.
OTS	No. Conducts informal benchmark surveys as needed.	N/A	N/A	N/A
SEC	No	N/A	N/A	N/A

Source: GAO summary of agency data.

The remaining three regulators (CFTC, OTS, and SEC) have participated in the pay and benefits surveys of other agencies, and officials from these agencies said that they have used the results of these surveys, but have not conducted their own. For example, an SEC official told us that his agency often uses FDIC's data because, like SEC, FDIC has a large number of compliance examiners and must negotiate pay and benefits with the same union as SEC. In 2002 and 2003, CFTC has also hired consultants to review existing surveys from FDIC and OCC as well as from information gathered from other regulators.

The agencies hired external compensation consultants to conduct the surveys because, according to officials from FCA and FDIC, these consultants provide an objective view of their agencies' pay and benefits. And, because they have often worked with other FIRREA agencies, the consultants can provide insights and perspectives based on information from other agencies. For pay comparability surveys, external compensation consultants compare base pay ranges for a given occupation, locality pay percentages and, to a lesser extent, annual bonus and other cash award policies. To compare pay across agencies, consultants send questionnaires on behalf of the sponsoring agency and ask participating agencies to match the jobs based on the job descriptions provided. The job descriptions usually contain information on duties, scope of responsibilities, and educational requirements. External compensation consultants also have used various methods to assess the comparability of benefits. For example, the consultant for FDIC did a side-by-side comparison of benefits offered at other agencies, and also calculated the total cost of benefits per employee.

In addition to conducting comparability surveys, agency officials told us that human capital officials at the 10 regulators have formed an interagency Financial Regulatory Agency Group. The members regularly consult with each other on pay and benefits issues, and as they prepare their budgets for the coming year, they meet to exchange information on potential and actual changes to pay and benefits. For example, the group has exchanged information on updates in merit pay ranges, bonuses, salary pay caps, and benefits such as flexible work schedules. Agency officials also have taken turns to update a spreadsheet that lists the pay ranges and benefits for all 10 financial regulators, a key document the agencies use to compare pay and especially benefits informally across agencies.

However, in consulting with each other to meet comparability requirements, agency officials told us that because many of the financial regulators conduct comparability surveys, their staffs have had to respond to numerous and often overlapping inquiries, which can be burdensome and inefficient. This is especially the case for smaller agencies, such as FCA and FHFB, which tend to have smaller human capital (personnel) departments than larger agencies that may have pay and benefits specialists who can handle comparability issues full time, including filling out and processing various comparability surveys. According to officials from a few regulators, partly as a result of the substantial investment of time and resources, some agencies have not been timely or forthcoming in sharing their pay and benefits information.

REGULATORS ARE EXPLORING THE FEASIBILITY OF A COMMON SURVEY

According to several agency officials, in response to renewed interest of upper management from several agencies in consolidating pay and benefits surveys, the regulators are studying the feasibility of such a method. In December 2006, the regulators formed a subcommittee within the Financial Regulatory Agency Group to study the feasibility of a common survey. Agency officials are exploring whether consolidating the various comparability surveys into a common survey will improve the process for job matching and result in more efficient use of resources. They also told us that the subcommittee also has discussed the feasibility of establishing a Web-based data system to make the most current pay and benefits information available to participating agencies. The subcommittee is working on the details of allocating costs of a common survey among the agencies, but has suggested that costs might be prorated based on the size of each regulatory agency. As of March 2007, agency officials had not yet received cost figures from potential consultants.

Agency officials who attended the first subcommittee meeting told us that implementation of a common survey would require collaboration and agreement on a number of matters, such as

- choice of external compensation consultant to conduct the common survey, since different consultants have different approaches to carry out the common survey;
- group of jobs to be benchmarked for the common survey and best approach for job matching, as some jobs are unique to certain agencies;
- timing and frequency of the common survey to meet everyone's needs since agencies determine pay and benefits at different times of the year and would need the updated information when the need arises;
- number and types of organizations to include in the common survey because while all agencies would want to include the financial regulators, some may need information from certain private-sector entities; and,
- cost of the common survey may be substantial, which according to some agencies, is a potential concern.

By forming the subcommittee to explore issues associated with developing a common survey, agency officials have adopted some of the practices that we identified that would enhance and sustain collaborative efforts. These practices include defining and articulating a common outcome, establishing means to operate across agency boundaries, and leveraging resources.[3]

Agency officials who are members of the subcommittee told us that the officials have sent a formal request for information to several consultant candidates. The request inquired about the consultants' ability to plan and execute a common survey that will provide customizable reports for each agency and also create a secure, centralized data source on pay and benefits. In addition, agency officials asked how the consultants would approach job matching, a complicated task. For example, officials from FDIC, OFHEO, and SEC told us that the use of different pay plans and grades among agencies and the location of field offices in cities with different employment market conditions contributed to the difficulty in matching jobs across regulators. In addition, some agency officials said that it is difficult to match jobs because agencies have different job requirements that may differ even when a job title is the same. The subcommittee received responses from various consultants and as of March 2007 was in the process of contacting the consultants to gather more details and to discuss the options available to them.

Most Regulators Used Benchmarks Developed from Surveys and Other Data to Assess Comparability and Make Adjustments to Pay and Benefits

In the absence of a legislative definition, agency officials told us that agencies have used various benchmarks, as shown in table 6, to assess pay and benefits comparability. For example, FDIC has sought to set its total pay ranges (base pay plus locality pay) for specific occupations and grade levels within 10 percent of the average of FIRREA agencies, a benchmark that pay and benefits consultants have used in their comparability surveys. FCA uses benchmarks, including average market rate paid by other financial regulators. CFTC uses average payroll and salary structure relative to other regulators. FHFB, NCUA, OTS, and SEC told us that they have not used specific benchmarks, and OTS uses informal benchmarks as needed.

Agency officials told us that all agencies, including the three agencies that have not conducted formal benefits surveys, have assessed their benefits comparability by comparing individual benefit items as well as agency contributions to specific benefits. They added that most agencies have used the interagency group spreadsheet that lists all the benefits and agency contributions offered.

Table 6. Selected Examples of Benchmarks Agencies Have Used to Assess Pay and Benefits Comparability

Agencies	Benchmark examples used to assess pay comparability	Benchmark examples used to assess benefits
CFTC	Average payroll, salary structure, etc., relative to other regulators.	Benefits being of similar types, and relative benefits costs as percentage of payroll.
FCA	Pay at average market rate paid by other financial regulators. The goal is to be in the middle range of the financial regulators.	No specific benchmarks.
FDIC	Since 1999, total pay (base pay plus locality pay) within 10 percent of the average of FIRREA agencies. Prior to 1999, no specific benchmarks were used.	Benefits being of similar types and having equivalent or similar overall value, without necessarily being identical.
FHFB	No specific benchmarks.	No specific benchmarks.
Federal Reserve Board	Pay at the average of the market, including regulators and other appropriate competitors.	Benefits being similar types.
NCUA	No specific benchmarks.	No specific benchmarks.
OCC	Pay within 10 percent of the other agencies' (or the market's) median base pay plus locality pay for each occupation and grade.	Benefits being similar types. OCC does not consider the cost of benefits.
OFHEO	Pay within 10 percent of average salary of other agencies or market average for each occupation and grade.	Benefits being of similar types and having equivalent or similar overall value, without necessarily being identical.
OTS	No specific benchmarks. Informal benchmarks as needed.	No specific benchmarks. Informal benchmarks as needed.
SEC	No specific benchmarks.	No specific benchmarks.

Source: GAO summary of agency information.

According to agency officials, the financial regulators have used information from the pay and benefits comparability surveys and discussions among the agencies in their efforts to seek to maintain comparability. Table 7 provides some recent examples of these efforts.

Table 7. Selected Examples of Recent Pay and Benefits Adjustments Resulting from Agencies' Comparability Assessments

Year	Action taken to adjust pay and benefits
2002	FCA adjusted its pay ranges based on its comparability survey, which stated that FCA's pay was lower than other FIRREA agencies.
2002	In response to recently enacted comparability requirements, SEC substantially increased its pay ranges to be comparable to those offered at other FIRREA agencies.
2003	As a result of gaining pay flexibilities, CFTC implemented new pay ranges for its 2003 pay schedule; CFTC increased base pay by 20 percent for all eligible employees to partially close the 25 percent gap between CFTC and FIRREA agencies.
2006	OFHEO increased its pay ranges across the board based on the findings from its 2005 pay and benefits survey.
2006	The FDIC increased its pay scale minimums by 1.5 percent and pay scale maximums by 6 percent, effective February 18, 2006, based on FDIC's consultant's analysis of its pay and benefits survey.

Source: GAO analysis of agency information.

Agency Pay and Benefits Policies and Several Other Factors Contribute to Variations in Pay and Benefits

Although the financial regulators have adjusted their pay and benefits to seek to maintain comparability, several factors influence compensation decisions that lead to some variations in pay ranges and benefit packages. As shown in figure 3 in the report, with the exception of the Federal Reserve Board and OFHEO, the financial regulators' total pay ranges consist of base pay and locality pay percentages that are calculated based on the employees' duty station. The Federal Reserve Board and OFHEO do not have separate locality pay percentages because Washington, D.C., is their only duty station. Figure 3 also shows that, for examiners, FDIC and NCUA pay ranges generally have lower minimum base pay than other agencies, and FDIC and OCC have higher maximum base pay for examiners. In addition, for economists, CFTC and FDIC pay ranges have lower minimum base pay than other agencies, and the CFTC and OCC pay ranges have higher maximum base pay.[4]

Actual average base pay figures that we obtained from the Central Personnel Data File and from the Federal Reserve Board also vary among the 10 agencies in relation to the agencies' respective base pay ranges, as shown in figure 3 in the report. For example, the actual average base pay for examiners at OCC ($92,371) is 52 percent of the maximum pay range of $177,600. However, actual average base pay as a percentage of maximum pay can vary considerably, as in the case of SEC attorneys. Their actual average base pay ($124,379) is 98 percent of the maximum pay range of $126,987.

According to agency officials, two factors affect where actual average base pay falls within an agency's pay range. One is the distribution of the length of service among employees. For example, the actual average base pay for agencies with a higher proportion of long-tenured employees would be closer to the maximum of its pay range. Conversely, actual average base pay for agencies with a higher proportion of new hires would fall closer to the minimum of the pay scale. An OCC official told us that despite the fact that OCC also has a large number of experienced examiners, the actual average pay for OCC examiners may seem low compared to other agencies because OCC has hired a large number of examiners during the last 2 years. Officials from several federal regulators also told us that they rarely hire at the lower grade level for some occupations. For example, FHFB tends to hire mid-level employees because its relatively small office cannot afford a long training period for new hires.

Table 8. Agencies' Current Methods for Determining Locality Pay Percentages and Adjustments

Agency	Methods for determining locality pay percentages and adjustments
CFTC	Uses OPM locality percentages.
FCA	Uses the average rate of 5 FIRREA agencies: FDIC, FHFB, NCUA, OCC, and OTS.
FDIC	Uses a formula jointly developed by the National Treasury Employees Union and FDIC primarily based on the Bureau of Labor Statistics National Compensation Survey Cost of Labor data for federally defined locality pay areas, with Runzheimer International cost of living data influence for a very few areas where there are extreme differences between cost of living and cost of labor.
FHFB	For Washington, D.C., considers other federal bank regulatory agencies per FHFB's comparability statute. For other locations, uses FDIC locality pay percentages.
Federal Reserve Board	Not Applicable. Washington, D.C., is the only duty station.
NCUA	Considers other FIRREA agencies.
OCC	Uses primarily cost of labor data from the Economic Research Institute.
OFHEO	Not Applicable. Washington, D.C., is the only duty station.
OTS	Uses Runzheimer International cost of living data.
SEC	Currently adjusts yearly locality pay percentage increases by at least the minimum recommended OPM locality incremental adjustment.

Source: GAO analysis of agency information.

As shown in table 2 in the report, locality pay percentages vary among agencies for the same duty station. Table 8 shows the methods that agencies are currently using to determine their respective locality pay percentages and adjustments.

Table 9. List of Benefits Offered by the 10 Financial Regulators

Benefit	CFTC	FCA	FDIC	FHFB
Insurance				
Health *(through OPM's Federal Employees Health Benefits program)*	Yes--agency pays 100% for reservists called to active duty	Yes--agency pays 70%	Yes--agency pays 85 - 88.75%	Yes--agency pays 85%
Dental *(through OPM's Federal Employees Dental and Vision Insurance program as of January 2007)*	Yes	Yes	Yes	Yes
Dental *(through agency)*	Yes--agency pays 100% of premium, annual limit of $1,500	No	Yes--agency pays 80% (beginning in January 2007)	Yes--agency pays 100%, annual limit of $2,000
Vision *(through OPM's Federal Employees Dental and Vision Insurance program as of January 2007)*	Yes	Yes	Yes	Yes
Vision *(through agency)*	No	No	Yes--agency pays 80% (beginning in January 2007)	Yes--agency pays 100%
Life *(through OPM's Federal Employees' Group Life Insurance program)*	Yes	Yes	Yes	Yes
Life *(through agency)*	No	No	Yes--agency pays 100%, if employee waives FEGLI; limit is $800,000	No
Long-term care *(through OPM's Federal Long Term Care Insurance program)*	Yes	Yes	Yes	Yes
Long-term care *(through agency)*	No	No	No	No

Table 9. (Continued)

Federal Reserve Board	NCUA	OCC	OFHEO	OTS	SEC
Yes--agency pays 72% on average	Yes	Yes--agency pays 72% plus $25 subsidy per pay period	Yes--agency pays 90%	Yes--agency pays $300	Yes--agency pays $25 or $50 subsidy per pay period for self only or self and family coverage, respectively
Yes	Yes	Yes	Yes	Yes	Yes
Yes--agency pays 80%, annual limit of $1,000 to $3,000, depending on plan, beginning January 2007	No	Yes--agency pays 100%, annual limit of $2,500	Yes--agency pays 100%, annual limit of $2,500	No	Yes--agency pays 100% of monthly premiums
Yes	Yes	Yes	Yes	Yes	Yes
Yes--agency pays 50% of premium (beginning in January 2007), employees pay $15 copay	No	Yes--agency pays 100% of premiums	Yes--agency pays 100% of premiums, employees pay $10 copay	No	Yes--agency pays 100% of monthly premiums
Yes	Yes	Yes	Yes	Yes	Yes
Yes--basic rate (of $.44 per $1,000) is subsidized 1/3 through agency; also, personal accident insurance is provided - employee pays 100%	No	Yes--agency contributes to cost, if employee waives FEGLI	No	Yes--agency pays 100%; employee pays 100% of optional coverage	No
Yes	Yes	Yes	Yes	Yes	Yes
Yes	No	No	No	No	No

Table 9. (Continued)

Benefit	CFTC	FCA	FDIC	FHFB
Long-term disability	No	Yes--benefit is 60% of employee monthly earnings, $100/month with limit of $8,000/month	Yes--agency pays 100% for standard option, employee pays some for high option	No
Short-term disability	No	No	No	No
Domestic partner health benefits	No	No	No	No
Business travel insurance (employer paid)	No	Yes	Yes	No
Prepaid legal/professional liability insurance	Yes--professional liability insurance for managers where agency pays 50% of premiums up to $200/year	Yes--employee pays 100%	No	No
Cafeteria plan	No	No	Includes FDIC's dental, vision, life, long-term disability, and health care and dependent-care flexible spending accounts	No
Other	No	No	No	No
Pre-Tax				
Pre-tax health premiums *(through OPM's Federal Employees Health Benefits program or agency programs)*	Yes--for FEHB	Yes--70 to 75% depending on the cost of the employee's health plan	Yes--for FEHB; agency dental, vision, and long term disability. Beginning in January 2007, dental and vision premiums through OPM's program will also be on a pre-tax basis	Yes--for FEHB

Table 9. (Continued)

Federal Reserve Board	NCUA	OCC	OFHEO	OTS	SEC
Yes--agency pays 60% of employee salary	No	Yes--agency pays 100%, limit of $10,000/month	No	Yes--agency pays 100%	No
No	No	Yes	No	No	No
Yes--agency reimburses up to 72% of cost of individual outside premium for domestic partner	No	Yes	No	No	No
Yes--agency pays 100%, $500,000 maximum	No	Yes--agency pays 100%, $750,000 maximum	No	Yes--agency pays 100%	No
Yes--employee pays 100%	No	Yes--$150 for professional liability insurance	Yes--up to $150 per year for professional liability insurance	No	Yes—professional liability insurance where agency pays 50% of premium toward private insurance
No	No	No	No	No	No
Yes--agency offers homeowners, liability, automobile, and boat insurance; personal accident, employee pays 100%	No	No	No	No	No
Yes--for FEHB, FEDVIP, agency dental and vision	Yes	Yes--for FEHB	Yes	Yes	Yes--for FEHB

Table 9. (Continued)

Benefit	CFTC	FCA	FDIC	FHFB
Dependent care flexible spending account *(through OPM's flexible spending account program)*	Yes	Yes	No--but employees may participate in the FDIC flexible spending account, same dollar limits as OPM's program	Yes
Health care flexible spending account *(through OPM's flexible spending account program)*	Yes	Yes	No--but employees may participate in FDIC flexible spending account, same dollar limits as OPM's program	Yes
Pre-tax agency contribution	No	$750 to be allocated between dependent care and health care accounts	No	No
Other				
Child care				
Child care centers --available on-site	No	No	Yes--at the Virginia Square and headquarters office	No
Child care subsidy	No	Yes--ranges from 25 - 70%, depending on income	No	No
Other	No	No	No	No

Table 9. (Continued)

Federal Reserve Board	NCUA	OCC	OFHEO	OTS	SEC
No--but employees may participate in the FRB flexible spending account, same dollar limits as OPM's program	Yes	No--but employees may participate in the OCC flexible spending account, same dollar limits as OPM's program	Yes	No--but employees may participate in the OTS flexible spending account	Yes
No--but employees may participate in FRB flexible spending account, same dollar limits as OPM's program	Yes	No--but employees may participate in OCC flexible spending account, same dollar limits as OPM's program	Yes	No--but employees may participate in the OTS flexible spending account	Yes
Dependent care credit of $1,000 for employees enrolled in dependent care flexible spending account earning less than $100,000 (effective January 2007)	No	No	No	OTS provides credit of $1,000	No
		Parking flexible spending account. Employees may set aside up to $215 for qualified parking expenses			
No	No	No	No--but available on-site through OTS	Yes--but not subsidized	No--but opening in fall 2007
No	No	No	No	No	Yes--ranges from 20 - 50%, depending on income
Dependent care referral service and subsidized back-up and emergency care covering both children and adults (beginning January 2007)	No	No	No	No	Subsidized back-up childcare

Table 9. (Continued)

Benefit	CFTC	FCA	FDIC	FHFB
Leave				
Annual leave *(same accrual rate as federal government, unless noted)*	Yes	Yes	Yes--but senior executives may accrue 8 hours/pay period without regard to years of service	Yes--but senior executives may accrue 8 hours/pay period without regard to years of service
Sick leave - personal and family *(same accrual rate as federal government, unless noted)*	Yes	Yes	Yes	Yes
Time-off awards	Yes	Yes	Yes	Yes
Credit time	Yes	Yes	Yes	Yes
Family and Medical Leave Act *(up to 12 weeks of unpaid leave per year)*	Yes	Yes	Yes	Yes
Compensatory time	Yes--for approved extra work hours, official travel, etc., within OPM and agency limits	Yes	Yes	Yes
Other	OPM Maternity/ paternity leave, leave-sharing program	Leave-sharing program	Leave-donation program	No
Travel and Relocation				
Transit benefits	Yes	Yes	Yes	Yes
Travel expenses	Yes	Yes	Yes	Yes
Relocation expenses	Yes	Yes	Yes	Yes
Home marketing incentive payments	Yes	Yes	No	No
Other	No		Yes--Loss on home sale, with deductible of 1st 5% of loss, and maximum of $20,000	Yes--Travel Impact Program where employees who travel more than 50 nights in fiscal year receive extra compensation
Educational and Professional Expenses				
Student loan repayment	No	Yes	No	Yes
Training (internal and external)	Yes	Yes	Yes	Yes

Table 9. (Continued)

Federal Reserve Board	NCUA	OCC	OFHEO	OTS	SEC
Yes	Yes	Yes--but senior executives may accrue 8 hours/pay period without regard to years of service	Yes	Yes	Yes
Yes	Yes	Yes	Yes	Yes	Yes
No	Yes	Yes	Yes	No	Yes
No	Yes	Yes	Yes	No	Yes
Yes	Yes	Yes	Yes	Yes	Yes
Yes	Yes	Yes	Yes	Yes--but used rarely	Yes
Emergency leave bank	No	Leave-sharing program	No	No	No
Yes	Yes	Yes	Yes	Yes	Yes
Yes	Yes	Yes	Yes	Yes	Yes
Yes--4-tier program based on employee position	Yes	Yes	Yes	Yes	Yes
Yes	No	Yes	No	No	No
		Yes--Travel Impact Program, loss on home sale; mortgage subsidy; renter subsidy; spouse/domestic partner career assistance; lease-breaking expense			No
No	No	No	No	No	Yes
Yes	Yes	Yes	Yes	Yes	Yes

Table 9. (Continued)

Benefit	CFTC	FCA	FDIC	FHFB
Academic degree training	No	Yes--if relevant to position	Yes--pilot MBA program for 10 candidates	No
Professional credential expenses	No	Yes	Yes--up to $250/year	Yes
Payment of professional organization fees/dues	No	Yes	Yes	Yes
Retirement				
Retirement (through OPM's Federal Employees Retirement System or Civil Service Retirement System	Yes	Yes	Yes	Yes
Retirement (*through agency)*	No	No	No	No
Phased retirement	No	No	No	No
Federal Thrift Savings Plan	Yes	Yes	Yes	Yes
Agency 401(k) plan	No	No--discontinued in December 2006	Yes--5% agency matching contribution	Yes--3% agency matching contribution
Disability retirement *(through OPM's program)*	Yes	Yes	Yes	Yes

Table 9. (Continued)

Federal Reserve Board	NCUA	OCC	OFHEO	OTS	SEC
Yes--if relevant to position; also reimbursement for books and certain fees	Yes--if relevant to position	Yes	No	Yes	Yes--if relevant to position
Yes--for bar dues, CPA exams, and bar review	No	Yes	Yes--but only for study programs and exams associated with position-related professional credentials	No	No
No	No	Yes	No	Yes	No
Yes--for certain positions	Yes	Yes	Yes	Yes	Yes
Yes--majority of employees are covered by the Federal Reserve System Plan. Agency pays 100% for employees hired after 12-31-1983; those hired before 1-1-1984 pay 7% of salary for a CSRS-like defined benefit plan that is not integrated with Social Security	No	No	No	Yes--for a grandfathered group of employees	No
No	No	No	No	No	No
No	Yes	Yes	Yes	Yes	Yes
Yes--$.80 on the $1 up to 6% agency matching contribution for the first 5 years of service; after that, $1 for $1 up to 6%	No	Yes--2% automatic agency contribution, additional 1% agency matching contribution	No	Yes--2% agency matching contribution for employees covered by FERS/CSRS, 7% match for employees under agency program	No
No	Yes	Yes	Yes	Yes	Yes

Table 9. (Continued)

Benefit	CFTC	FCA	FDIC	FHFB
Disability retirement *(through agency)*	No	No	No	No
Retiree health benefits *(through OPM's program)*	Yes	Yes	Yes	Yes
Retiree health benefits *(through agency)*	No	No	No	No
Retiree life insurance *(through OPM's program)*	Yes	Yes	Yes	Yes
Retiree life insurance *(through agency)*	No	No	Yes	No
Voluntary Early Retirement Authority	Yes	Yes	Yes	As necessary
Work/Life Benefit				
Alternative work schedules	Yes	Yes	Yes	Yes
Telework	Yes	Yes	Yes	Yes
Part-time work	Yes	Yes	Yes	Yes
Job sharing	No	Yes	Yes	No
Lifecycle or wellness account	No	Yes--$400 per year reimbursement of expenses related to adoption, fitness/recreation, insurance premiums, and child care and elder care	Yes--$250/year reimbursement of eligible expenses related to different life stages	Yes--$700/year reimbursement for physical fitness and health-related expenses
Parking	Yes--for limited senior staff and those with medical need	Yes--no-cost parking garages in all locations	Yes--free to senior executives in headquarters; for some locations, free for all other employees	Yes--on-site, reduced cost parking
Technology equipment or services (e.g., laptop computer, cellular phone, blackberry services, high-speed Internet at home)	Yes--for limited senior and continuity staff	Yes—high-speed Internet at home for business needs; blackberries, cellular phones to senior executives and others with business needs; laptop computer to all staff.	Yes--for senior executives; selected examiners participating in telework program receive reimbursements for multiple telephone lines or high-speed Internet.	Yes--for executives and certain emergency employees
Subsidized on-site cafeteria	No	Yes	Yes	No
Business casual dress	Yes	Yes	Yes	Yes
Retirement planning services	Yes	Yes	Yes	Yes

Table 9. (Continued)

Federal Reserve Board	NCUA	OCC	OFHEO	OTS	SEC
Yes	No	No	No	Yes	No
Yes	Yes	Yes	Yes	Yes	Yes
No	No	No	No	Yes	No
Yes	Yes	Yes	Yes	Yes	Yes
Yes (participants prior to 1-1- 2005 only)	No	Yes	No	Yes	No
Yes	No	Yes	No	No	No--expired in September 2006
Yes	Yes	Yes	Yes	Yes	Yes
Yes	Yes	Yes	Yes	Yes	Yes
Yes	Yes	Yes	Yes	Yes	Yes
Yes	No	Yes	No	No	Yes
No	No	Yes--$600 per year	No	No	No
Yes--limited based on position, requests, car pools	Yes	Yes--on-site reduced-cost parking;	Yes--but a limited number	Yes--but limited	Yes--for senior officers
Yes	Yes--dependent upon position	Yes	Yes--dependent upon position	Yes--but limited	Yes--but limited
Yes	No	Yes	No	No	No
Yes	Yes	Yes	Yes	Yes	Yes
Yes	Yes	Yes	No	No	Yes

Table 9. (Continued)

Benefit	CFTC	FCA	FDIC	FHFB
Employee assistance programs (e.g., counseling, referral services)	Yes	Yes	Yes	Yes
Physical exam program	Yes--a limited number of free exams annually	Yes--$150/year reimbursement for exams	No	No
Fitness centers	Yes--at headquarters and largest regional office	Yes--at headquarters	Yes--at headquarters and Virginia Square office	Yes
On-site defibrillator	No	Yes	Yes	Yes
On-site health unit	Yes	No	Yes--at headquarters and limited regional offices	No
Other medical services/exams	Yes	Yes--flu shots	Yes--annual health fair, flu shots, free screenings -- lipid profile, glaucoma, bone density, blood pressure, mammography, prostate, and skin cancer	No
Other Benefits and Payments				
Severance pay	Yes	Yes	Yes	Yes
Workers compensation	Yes	Yes	Yes	Yes
Death benefits	Yes	Yes	Yes	Yes
Survivor benefits	Yes	Yes	Yes	Yes
Voluntary Separation Incentive Payments	No	No	Yes	Yes--As necessary

Table 9. (Continued)

Federal Reserve Board	NCUA	OCC	OFHEO	OTS	SEC
Yes	Yes	Yes	Yes	Yes	Yes--plus 24-hour resource and referral service for all employees
Yes--free, on-site exams every years for employees over age 35	Yes--annual physical exam for senior staff; exam for other staff every 2 or 3 years depending on age	Yes--$200 or $300/year, depending on position; reimbursement for routine physical exam by a physician of their choice	No	No	Yes--annual physical exams at on-site health units
Yes	Yes	Yes--at headquarters	Yes	Yes	Yes--at headquarters locations
Yes	Yes	Yes	Yes	Yes	Yes
Yes	No	Yes--but limited to several times a week	No	No	Yes--at two headquarters locations
Yes	Yes--annual physical exam for senior staff; exams for other staff every one to three years	Yes--annual health fair, flu shot, screenings, blood pressure, and cholesterol	Yes--annual health fair with screenings for prostate cancer, cholesterol, and blood pressure	Yes--annual health fair	Yes--flu shots, other immunizations, smoking cessation, cardiac risk profiles, and health consultations
Yes	Yes	Yes	Yes	Yes	No
Yes	Yes	Yes	Yes	Yes	Yes
Yes	Yes	Yes	Yes	Yes	Yes
Yes	Yes	Yes	Yes	Yes	No
No	No	Yes—As necessary	No	No	Yes--limited through 9/30/07

Source: GAO analysis of agency data.

The benefits that the 10 financial regulators offered also varied. Although all of the agencies offer standard federal government benefits, there are variations in the extent of agency contributions and types of additional benefits these agencies offer. For example, all financial regulators offer the Federal Employees Health Benefits program, but agency contributions differ. Some agencies pay for a percentage of the health premium (e.g. 70 percent at FCA and 90 percent at OFHEO). CFTC contributes 100 percent for reservists called to active duty. The following are selected examples of the additional benefits that some financial regulators offer as of September 2006 unless noted otherwise:

- Five of the 10 regulators— FDIC, FHFB, the Federal Reserve Board, OCC, and OTS—offer their employees 401(k) retirement savings plans with varying employer contributions. In addition, all agencies except the Federal Reserve Board offer the federal Thrift Savings Plan.[5]
- The Federal Reserve Board and OCC offer domestic partner benefits for some types of plans.
- FCA and SEC offer child care subsidies, and FDIC and OTS offer on-site day care.
- FCA, FDIC, FHFB, and OCC reimburse employee expenses related to items such as fitness, recreation, and adoption in their wellness accounts. Amounts differ from $250 per year at FDIC to $700 per year at FHFB.

According to agency officials, a number of factors have influenced their pay and benefits policies and could have contributed to the variations in their pay ranges and benefits. For example, the length of time an agency has been under the comparability requirements and related compensation flexibility provisions affected compensation. CFTC and SEC officials told us that because their agencies received pay and benefits flexibilities and were put under a comparability requirement much later (in 2002) than the six FIRREA agencies (in 1989), CFTC and SEC have taken an incremental approach to slowly increase their pay and benefits to close the gap with the other financial regulators. According to a CFTC official, this would allow time for employee input and acceptance while building agency capacity to manage the authority. Budgetary constraints represent another factor. OFHEO officials told us that OFHEO did not implement a new 401(k) retirement savings plan recommended by its external compensation consultant, Watson Wyatt, in its 2005 comparability survey because OFHEO is working to control the growth of its personnel expenses and because budget limitations resulting from being part of the appropriations process has caused OFHEO to curtail new benefits programs. Furthermore, agency officials said that an agency has to consider the particular needs and preferences of the agency's workforce as well as ways to attract and retain its workforce. For example, CFTC added a fully paid dental benefit as a result of an online vote by employees on preferred benefits options. FDIC officials indicated that its employees greatly value the matching contribution FDIC provides on its 401(k) plan, and found that the matching contribution is also an effective retention tool. Similarly, OCC added a 401(k) retirement savings plan in order to attract and retain employees. According to an SEC official, SEC uses a student loan repayment benefit because the benefit helps to attract and retain employees, many of whom are recent law school graduates. Agency officials emphasized that it was not their goal to have identical pay and benefits packages; rather, they considered pay and benefits as a total package when seeking to maintain pay and benefits comparability and when setting pay and benefits policies aimed at recruiting and retaining employees. See table 9 for more detailed information on the benefits that the 10 financial regulators offer.

The previous table lists selected benefits identified by 10 financial regulators as of September 2006, unless otherwise noted in the table. We included the following categories of benefits: insurance, pre-tax benefits, child care, leave, travel and relocation, educational and professional expenses, retirement, work/life benefits, and other benefits and payments.

APPENDIX V. ANALYSIS OF MOVEMENT DATA OF FINANCIAL REGULATOR EMPLOYEES FROM FISCAL YEARS 1990 THROUGH 2006

We reviewed the movement of financial regulator employees from fiscal year 1990 through 2006 using data from the Central Personnel Data File (CPDF). We found that the movement of employees among the financial regulators was very low and presented no discernible trend, but that 86 percent (13,433 of the 15,627) of employees leaving the regulators voluntarily (i.e., moving or resigning) resigned from the federal government. Our analysis did not include the Federal Reserve Board of Governors because CPDF does not contain data from the Federal Reserve Board. (For more detail on our methodology, see app. I.) This appendix includes additional data for fiscal years 1990 through 2006 on the average number of these employees moving among the 9 financial regulators; the movement of employees among 9 of the 10 financial regulatory agencies by occupation; and employment by occupation and employee movement agency snapshots.

Figure 8 shows the average number of employees in mission-critical and other occupations moving among the 9 financial regulators for which we have data from fiscal year 1990 through fiscal year 2006. On average, a total of 919 employees per year moved or resigned. Movement ranged from an average of less than 1 for investigators to an average of over 11 for examiners.

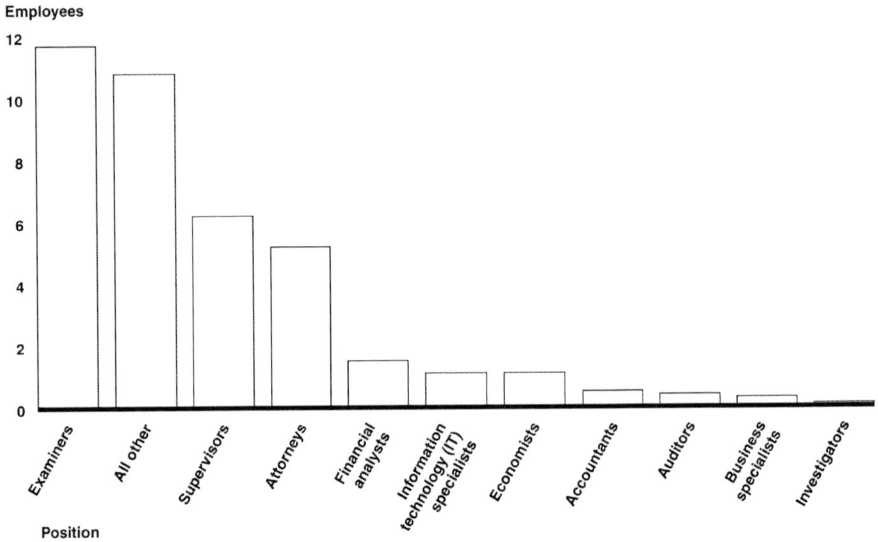

Source: GAO analysis of CPDF data.

Note: This table does not include data for the Federal Reserve Board because CPDF does not include data for the agency. The "all other" category combines specialists in occupations such as human resources management, administration, clerical, management and program analysis, financial administration, and paralegal work.

Figure 8. Average Number of Employees in Mission-Critical and other Occupations Moving among the 9 Financial Regulators, Fiscal Years 1990–2006.

Table 10 provides the actual number of financial regulator employees for whom we had data, by mission-critical and other occupations, who moved to another financial regulator from fiscal year 1990 through 2006.

Tables 11 through 19 provide employment by occupation and movement data for 9 of the 10 agencies from fiscal year 1990 through 2006.[1]

Table 10. Number of Financial Regulator Employees in Mission-Critical and Other Occupations Who Moved to Another Financial Regulator, Fiscal Years 1990–2006

Fiscal year	Accountant	Attorney	Auditor	Business Specialist	Economist	Examiner[d]	Financial Analyst	Investigator[c]	IT Specialist	Supervisor[a]	All other[b]	Total
1990	1	9	0	0	0	12	1	0	0	9	30	**62**
1991	0	19	0	0	1	12	4	0	3	21	37	**97**
1992	2	3	3	0	1	21	2	0	0	3	19	**54**
1993	0	3	0	1	0	15	1	0	1	3	8	**32**
1994	0	3	0	0	0	8	1	0	0	8	3	**23**
1995	0	3	0	0	1	6	2	0	0	13	11	**36**
1996	1	4	1	1	0	3	0	0	1	2	5	**18**
1997	0	3	0	0	1	2	1	0	1	7	1	**16**
1998	0	8	0	0	0	28	0	0	0	4	7	**47**
1999	0	5	0	0	0	14	4	0	2	2	8	**35**
2000	0	9	0	0	1	9	1	1	0	3	10	**34**
2001	1	3	0	1	2	15	1	0	2	2	9	**36**
2002	0	7	0	0	1	5	0	0	3	7	4	**27**
2003	1	3	0	1	1	2	2	0	0	3	6	**19**
2004	1	2	0	0	3	17	1	0	2	5	10	**41**
2005	0	1	2	1	6	14	2	0	4	5	7	**42**
2006	1	3	1	0	0	16	2	0	0	8	8	**39**

Source: GAO analysis of CPDF data.

Note: This table does not include data for the Federal Reserve Board.

[a]Supervisors included executives, who constituted less than 1 percent of all supervisors who moved to another financial regulator.

[b]The "all other" category, which combines specialists in occupations such as human resources management, administration, clerical, management and program analysis, financial administration, and paralegal work.

[c]CFTC officials told us that some employees in the investigation job series 1801 were examiners. Because the CPDF cannot distinguish employees in the same job series but in different job titles, we called all the CFTC employees classified as 1801 examiners and classified those in job series 1802 (compliance investigation and support) as investigators at CFTC.

[d]OFHEO officials told us that some employees in the job series 0501 (financial administration and program) were examiners; because of limitations of the CPDF we put all employees in job series 0501 into the examiner job series.

Table 11. Commodity Futures Trading Commission Employment and Movement Data, Fiscal Years 1990–2006

Employment and movement	1990	1991	1992	1993	1994	1995	1996	1997	1998	1999	2000	2001	2002	2003	2004	2005	2006
Employment																	
All employees	495	559	570	536	516	507	515	521	527	519	515	496	468	492	490	487	446
Accountant	0	0	0	0	0	0	1	1	1	0	0	0	0	1	1	1	1
Attorney	65	83	83	73	73	87	100	114	119	120	117	113	109	145	142	140	123
Auditor	27	29	27	26	24	25	24	25	26	26	27	25	23	23	23	26	26
Business Specialist	4	2	0	0	0	0	0	0	0	0	0	0	0	0	0	0	0
Economist	35	32	35	34	31	25	26	26	27	30	26	26	28	33	35	36	33
Examiner	47	64	69	66	66	70	73	66	61	66	68	66	59	57	62	61	59
Financial Analyst	1	1	1	1	1	1	1	1	1	3	4	4	4	3	3	3	3
Investigator	7	5	7	7	13	13	15	19	20	21	23	22	18	17	14	14	12
IT Specialist	15	15	16	15	16	16	17	19	21	23	25	28	24	28	30	29	29
All other	148	171	174	158	146	139	134	133	133	129	123	112	102	103	97	92	80
Supervisor	146	157	158	156	146	131	124	117	118	101	102	100	101	82	83	85	80
Movement																	
To other financial regulator	10	6	5	1	2	6	1	3	10	5	7	4	2	2	1	0	3
To other federal agency	16	10	5	6	1	4	2	12	11	12	6	14	8	5	0	3	7
Resigned	38	28	23	19	27	23	26	18	28	27	34	20	12	6	15	9	9
Retired	7	2	3	6	10	7	7	6	9	13	5	8	31	8	7	9	33
Fired, other separations, reductions in force	8	1	2	3	0	2	3	3	1	1	1	1	0	3	3	0	1

Source: GAO analysis of CPDF data.

Table 12. Farm Credit Administration Employment and Movement Data, Fiscal Years 1990-2006

Employment and movement	**1990**	**1991**	**1992**	**1993**	**1994**	**1995**	**1996**	**1997**	**1998**	**1999**	**2000**	**2001**	**2002**	**2003**	**2004**	**2005**	**2006**
Employment																	
All employees	493	491	458	427	398	371	321	290	287	289	269	263	258	266	275	252	248
Accountant	7	8	9	8	7	6	7	9	8	8	6	5	5	5	5	4	5
Attorney	11	17	16	12	11	10	9	9	10	11	11	13	11	11	11	11	12
Auditor	4	1	0	2	2	1	1	1	0	0	0	1	1	1	1	1	1
Economist	3	4	3	3	3	2	1	1	2	3	3	3	3	3	2	3	3
Examiner	243	219	216	193	176	165	140	126	125	124	115	110	108	113	122	114	115
Financial Analyst	12	14	10	9	8	7	6	4	5	5	6	6	7	6	7	5	2
Investigator	0	0	0	1	1	1	1	1	1	1	1	1	1	1	1	1	0
IT Specialist	21	23	22	23	27	24	21	22	21	22	20	17	18	15	17	17	15
All other	109	124	117	110	100	94	74	74	74	74	64	65	61	65	64	57	51
Supervisor	83	81	65	66	63	61	61	43	41	41	43	42	43	46	45	39	44
Movement																	
To other financial regulator	12	1	7	5	4	1	0	1	4	0	1	1	1	1	2	2	2
To other federal agency	7	9	16	2	1	2	4	7	1	3	7	4	3	1	0	4	3
Resigned	46	31	27	19	9	10	24	8	6	12	11	3	4	1	5	6	5
Retired	7	4	5	4	17	6	9	9	8	2	4	11	4	6	7	15	15
Fired, other separations, reductions in force	6	0	7	3	2	6	12	14	4	0	1	0	0	0	1	2	1

Source: GAO analysis of CPDF data.

Table 13. Federal Deposit Insurance Corporation Employment and Movement Data, Fiscal Years 1990–2006

Employment and movement	1990	1991	1992	1993	1994	1995	1996	1997	1998	1999	2000	2001	2002	2003	2004	2005	2006
Employment																	
All employees	7,839	9,429	9,863	9,564	9,061	8,438	7,662	6,813	6,616	6,627	6,386	6,212	5,822	5,384	5,259	4,516	4,328
Accountant	107	132	88	115	102	145	133	110	95	90	86	83	81	58	56	66	58
Attorney	464	613	604	525	539	476	405	336	291	299	269	261	210	203	203	187	175
Auditor	93	167	193	166	152	147	150	133	117	115	113	110	73	67	68	61	45
Business Specialist	204	212	122	62	50	65	41	57	55	52	56	234	250	253	242	83	78
Economist	17	15	11	12	12	13	12	27	34	39	37	37	41	39	36	37	42
Examiner	2,808	3,098	3,162	3,084	2,778	2,511	2,087	1,883	2,343	2,434	2,324	2,215	2,195	2,091	2,026	1,895	1,814
Financial Analyst	778	684	373	653	693	505	409	252	218	221	201	113	100	96	98	91	82
Investigator	4	45	57	54	45	43	38	31	28	27	31	36	33	30	34	32	33
IT Specialist	156	310	289	269	270	283	278	266	296	326	324	328	327	312	306	252	252
All other	1,985	2,510	2,780	2,706	2,569	2,750	2,760	2,506	2,008	1,942	1,903	1,827	1,693	1,490	1,474	1,181	1,136
Supervisor	1,223	1,643	2,184	1,918	1,851	1,500	1,349	1,212	1,131	1,082	1,042	968	819	745	716	631	613
Movement																	
To other financial regulator	5	3	9	7	1	5	6	1	21	14	5	10	15	3	11	22	17
To other federal agency	21	29	48	18	17	44	22	37	28	25	31	14	52	28	20	56	12
Resigned	340	384	412	426	432	344	662	487	200	171	200	134	212	98	89	182	103
Retired	38	56	73	58	96	71	389	229	161	110	140	116	464	123	105	453	144
Fired, other separations, reductions in force	26	24	21	30	50	55	22	61	66	32	52	21	51	55	25	74	17

Source: GAO analysis of CPDF data.

Note: During some of the time under review, FDIC was actively downsizing its workforce and achieved that in part by providing buyouts and other incentives for employees to leave.

Table 14. Federal Housing Finance Board Employment and Movement Data, Fiscal Years 1990–2006

Employment and movement	1990	1991	1992	1993	1994	1995	1996	1997	1998	1999	2000	2001	2002	2003	2004	2005	2006
Employment																	
All employees	53	90	96	97	90	91	102	101	104	107	100	97	101	85	94	81	122
Accountant	0	0	0	0	0	0	1	1	3	4	4	4	4	4	4	2	2
Attorney	2	0	3	2	2	2	2	2	8	10	5	7	5	4	3	6	6
Auditor	0	1	0	0	0	0	0	1	2	2	1	1	1	0	1	2	2
Business Specialist	0	0	0	0	0	0	0	0	1	1	0	0	1	0	0	0	0
Economist	1	0	0	0	0	0	0	0	1	3	3	7	8	5	4	1	7
Examiner	0	0	0	0	0	0	0	0	0	8	9	9	11	17	17	27	36
Financial Analyst	3	8	10	7	5	7	6	5	20	10	11	11	10	11	15	10	21
IT Specialist	0	1	1	1	1	2	2	2	3	3	5	5	5	2	2	0	2
All other	28	35	34	37	35	30	35	30	45	47	38	37	38	19	19	19	24
Supervisor	19	45	48	50	47	50	56	60	21	19	24	16	18	23	29	14	22
Movement																	
To other financial regulator	0	1	1	0	1	1	0	2	0	3	1	2	1	0	4	2	4
To other federal agency	0	6	3	1	0	0	0	1	6	1	2	4	3	6	2	2	1
Resigned	4	1	6	10	13	10	3	2	4	4	7	4	5	2	3	3	4
Retired	1	0	0	0	1	0	2	1	1	1	19	0	4	4	2	3	3
Fired, other separations, reductions in force	1	0	0	1	0	2	2	2	1	0	3	1	0	13	1	0	0

Source: GAO analysis of CPDF data.

Table 15. National Credit Union Administration Employment and Employee Movement Data, Fiscal Years 1990–2006

Employment and movement	1990	1991	1992	1993	1994	1995	1996	1997	1998	1999	2000	2001	2002	2003	2004	2005	2006
Employment																	
All employees	717	917	907	909	876	878	890	883	838	930	954	936	946	918	890	896	919
Accountant	1	2	1	1	4	5	4	2	2	4	4	4	4	4	3	4	5
Attorney	5	4	2	2	12	14	13	14	14	16	16	16	16	16	14	17	17
Auditor	458	667	655	636	599	526	429	8	5	6	4	5	4	3	4	3	3
Economist	1	1	0	0	1	0	0	0	0	0	0	0	0	0	0	1	1
Examiner	18	17	10	11	3	81	203	684	655	723	734	718	689	607	595	584	607
Financial Analyst	1	1	1	1	3	6	6	7	7	7	9	9	8	7	7	6	5
Investigator	1	1	1	1	1	1	1	1	1	2	2	2	2	2	2	2	2
IT Specialist	1	23	18	16	23	25	24	20	19	23	23	28	28	27	28	25	27
All other	107	123	129	129	125	124	125	120	112	131	130	128	131	122	113	121	125
Supervisor	124	78	90	112	105	96	85	27	23	18	32	26	64	130	124	133	127
Movement																	
To other financial regulator	0	5	2	0	1	0	1	0	1	1	1	0	2	0	2	2	1
To other federal agency	2	7	3	1	4	4	4	3	9	4	6	6	4	5	2	3	4
Resigned	38	36	23	22	28	34	35	49	55	42	39	30	15	12	15	27	24
Retired	11	9	6	3	17	18	7	14	20	10	15	15	16	18	33	37	17
Fired, other separations, reductions in force	1	5	5	9	10	4	3	5	5	7	6	4	3	3	14	9	8

Source: GAO analysis of CPDF data.

Table 16. Office of the Comptroller of the Currency Employment and Employee Movement Data, Fiscal Years 1990–2006

Employment and movement	1990	1991	1992	1993	1994	1995	1996	1997	1998	1999	2000	2001	2002	2003	2004	2005	2006
Employment																	
All employees	3,218	3,344	3,628	3,962	3,898	3,573	3,297	2,742	2,862	2,917	2,781	2,819	2,780	2,748	2,686	2,768	2,908
Accountant	18	15	15	22	19	23	25	24	25	26	18	21	26	26	23	22	16
Attorney	79	89	89	94	95	109	99	92	99	98	98	89	94	93	91	93	98
Business Specialist	2	2	2	2	1	1	1	1	1	1	0	0	0	0	0	0	1
Economist	12	21	23	23	30	36	37	34	34	36	31	31	28	30	29	29	34
Examiner	2,076	2,161	2,393	2,685	2,598	2,245	1,997	1,622	1,734	1,735	1,708	1,760	1,719	1,720	1,685	1,762	1,864
Financial Analyst	10	13	13	15	16	17	17	17	20	18	13	11	11	12	11	10	13
IT Specialist	82	91	99	114	115	124	125	112	120	137	126	126	121	107	104	101	109
All other	555	598	631	664	679	673	651	553	580	607	537	531	537	508	502	523	537
Supervisor	384	354	363	343	345	345	345	287	249	259	250	250	244	252	241	228	236
Movement																	
To other financial regulator	9	5	5	3	1	6	3	2	2	7	10	7	5	9	14	8	5
To other federal agency	15	16	12	11	7	7	4	6	6	14	17	23	8	23	8	14	16
Resigned	216	164	195	196	233	298	256	394	156	115	159	122	80	71	78	73	91
Retired	18	33	14	13	21	100	23	179	30	20	88	45	29	39	86	50	50
Fired, other separations, reductions in force	9	13	19	15	18	11	31	10	4	11	13	14	10	8	18	2	9

Source: GAO analysis of CPDF data.

Table 17. Office of Federal Housing Enterprise Oversight Employment and Employee Movement Data, Fiscal Years 1990–2006

Employment and movement	1990	1991	1992	1993	1994	1995	1996	1997	1998	1999	2000	2001	2002	2003	2004	2005	2006
Employment																	
All employees	0	0	0	0	35	61	62	61	61	68	89	109	110	137	139	192	204
Accountant	0	0	0	0	0	0	0	0	0	0	0	0	0	0	4	4	13
Attorney	0	0	0	0	3	5	5	6	6	6	6	9	5	5	5	4	4
Business Specialist	0	0	0	0	0	0	0	0	0	0	0	0	1	1	1	1	0
Economist	0	0	0	0	2	6	7	4	3	1	2	1	0	0	1	1	1
Examiner	0	0	0	0	2	3	5	5	3	3	3	3	28	35	38	64	62
Financial Analyst	0	0	0	0	2	4	1	2	4	2	2	2	0	0	0	0	0
IT Specialist	0	0	0	0	18	27	28	31	30	39	61	75	27	40	41	58	64
All other	0	0	0	0	5	14	14	13	14	16	15	16	19	23	21	24	23
Supervisor	0	0	0	0	3	2	2	0	1	1	0	3	30	33	28	36	37
Movement																	
To other financial regulator	0	0	0	0	0	0	1	1	0	1	0	3	0	0	2	1	0
To other federal agency	0	0	0	0	0	0	0	3	3	3	0	0	0	1	1	1	4
Resigned	0	0	0	0	2	5	7	6	9	2	6	4	2	4	8	6	6
Retired	0	0	0	0	0	0	0	1	0	0	0	0	2	1	3	2	4
Fired, other separations, reductions in force	0	0	0	0	0	0	0	1	0	0	1	0	2	0	2	1	4

Source: GAO analysis of CPDF data.

Table 18. Office of Thrift Supervision Employment and Employee Movement Data, Fiscal Years 1990–2006

Employment and movement	1990	1991	1992	1993	1994	1995	1996	1997	1998	1999	2000	2001	2002	2003	2004	2005	2006
Employment																	
All employees	3,167	2,642	2,378	2,047	1,755	1,481	1,388	1,302	1,253	1,278	1,244	1,183	937	899	872	898	956
Accountant	13	42	38	35	14	13	10	10	8	8	8	8	7	10	8	10	10
Attorney	64	166	168	149	72	57	50	46	43	41	38	28	22	20	18	18	19
Specialist	6	31	22	22	6	6	6	7	8	14	17	13	12	8	6	6	6
Economist	4	4	7	7	6	6	5	6	6	7	6	5	5	4	2	3	3
Examiner	0	1,175	1,071	937	764	645	594	546	515	537	514	554	488	469	461	467	499
Financial Analyst	13	112	104	81	61	51	48	44	44	42	42	38	22	26	26	27	27
Investigator	2	0	0	0	0	0	0	0	0	0	0	0	0	0	0	0	0
IT Specialist	47	50	55	48	35	37	36	35	38	39	40	39	35	47	49	47	50
All other	2,881	1,059	911	767	478	389	370	358	352	357	350	278	184	168	157	166	176
Supervisor	137	3	2	1	319	277	269	250	239	233	229	220	162	147	145	154	166
Movement																	
To other financial regulator	20	66	22	14	12	11	5	2	7	3	5	7	1	4	4	3	2
To other federal agency	11	17	10	6	6	13	2	3	4	2	8	8	6	1	0	0	3
Resigned	33	218	201	190	198	152	81	55	41	21	51	30	12	5	9	10	15
Retired	5	67	25	119	19	33	19	19	26	32	34	53	146	28	29	27	33
Fired, other separations, reductions in force	3	35	59	36	42	25	2	5	5	3	10	14	76	1	4	1	4

Source: GAO analysis of CPDF data.

Table 19. Securities and Exchange Commission Employment and Employee Movement Data, Fiscal Years 1990–2006

Employment and movement	1990	1991	1992	1993	1994	1995	1996	1997	1998	1999	2000	2001	2002	2003	2004	2005	2006
Employment																	
All employees	2,214	2,324	2,540	2,614	2,603	2,719	2,694	2,687	2,656	2,711	2,806	2,914	2,930	3,121	3,589	3,727	3,488
Accountant	121	143	159	328	330	334	340	346	335	358	379	409	452	523	668	730	709
Attorney	474	520	558	577	577	625	641	644	674	688	784	875	960	1,057	1,144	1,124	1,023
Auditor	3	3	0	1	2	3	3	2	3	2	1	2	2	0	0	0	1
Business Specialist	0	0	1	1	1	1	1	1	0	0	1	1	1	2	2	23	19
Economist	9	6	6	7	7	6	6	3	6	8	17	18	15	17	19	18	18
Examiner	175	193	255	117	151	184	192	195	174	193	178	179	148	158	244	207	149
Financial Analyst	42	38	34	18	17	16	12	13	12	8	8	7	8	8	10	7	6
Investigator	16	17	31	36	40	39	38	40	34	35	37	36	32	32	32	33	32
IT Specialist	58	64	79	97	102	113	110	111	96	115	119	118	130	135	136	178	166
All other	723	716	740	722	690	690	665	660	649	634	631	642	620	610	641	649	627
Supervisor	593	624	677	710	686	708	686	672	673	670	651	627	562	579	693	758	738
Movement																	
To other financial regulator	6	10	3	2	1	6	1	4	2	1	4	2	0	0	1	2	5
To other federal agency	41	34	17	9	12	16	16	24	35	30	35	37	21	20	19	20	20
Resigned	210	142	134	137	186	186	207	231	240	188	291	168	106	107	144	189	207
Retired	29	20	13	21	28	43	32	42	47	37	24	21	18	29	22	60	64
Fired, other separations, reductions in force	13	9	2	5	28	7	6	10	4	12	7	3	5	5	7	16	8

Source: GAO analysis of CPDF data.

Table 20. Other Federal Agencies Employment and Employee Movement Data, Fiscal Years 1990–2006

Employment and movement	1990	1991	1992	1993	1994	1995	1996	1997
Employment								
All employees	1,943,615	1,959,655	1,963,728	1,905,028	1,835,449	1,766,783	1,717,727	1,658,155
Accountant	7,632	7,948	8,210	8,168	8,393	8,609	8,715	8,700
Attorney	12,910	13,941	14,787	15,082	15,183	16,193	16,626	16,821
Auditor	10,693	10,611	10,415	10,262	10,058	10,078	9,801	9,527
Business Specialist	12,056	12,535	12,937	12,991	13,140	14,902	15,182	14,836
Economist	3,346	3,544	3,655	3,523	3,509	3,566	3,554	3,570
Examiner	0	1	1	2	2	2	2	2
Financial Analyst	606	752	795	778	84	733	770	793
Investigator	31,070	32,286	33,379	33,685	34,981	37,307	39,828	40,980
IT Specialist	39,689	41,291	43,275	43,890	44,348	45,448	45,953	45,758
All other	1,516,871	1,521,230	1,515,467	1,461,878	1,413,323	1,364,824	1,327,893	1,281,480
Supervisor	308,742	315,516	320,807	314,769	291,728	265,121	249,403	235,688
Movement								
To financial regulator	497	544	359	198	130	64	57	103
To other federal agency	17,233	25,209	17,356	15,052	12,643	14,125	12,150	13,515
Resigned	81,585	64,794	56,279	56,937	50,928	49,707	49,164	51,756
Retired	42,321	43,176	28,809	59,379	65,587	69,628	50,777	55,729
Fired, other separations, reductions in force	16,642	19,674	16,926	16,762	19,126	18,540	21,765	16,109

Table 20. (Continued)

Employment and movement	1998	1999	2000	2001	2002	2003	2004	2005	2006
Employment									
All employees	1,628,983	1,607,983	1,601,565	1,617,526	1,669,546	1,679,585	1,700,009	1,699,504	1,696,480
Accountant	8,580	8,675	8,616	8,815	8,841	8,913	8,834	9,145	9,133
Attorney	17,300	17,959	18,157	18,775	19,062	19,286	19,693	19,915	20,453
Auditor	9,181	8,875	8,919	8,754	9,099	9,099	8,935	8,775	8,686
Business Specialist	15,173	15,491	16,135	16,830	17,075	17,399	17,561	17,904	17,970
Economist	3,671	3,381	3,389	3,443	3,527	3,697	3,719	3,728	3,281
Examiner	1	1	1	0	0	1	0	0	0
Financial Analyst	872	914	868	897	890	932	912	919	924
Investigator	43,561	44,095	44,122	44,596	50,738	52,127	52,774	54,517	99,211
IT Specialist	46,264	46,699	47,888	51,863	55,851	57,465	57,683	58,085	57,055
All other	1,257,499	1,239,770	1,232,771	1,244,012	1,281,032	1,287,270	1,304,224	1,298,809	1,250,843
Supervisor	226,881	222,123	220,699	219,541	223,431	223,396	225,674	227,707	228,924
Movement									
To financial regulator	154	177	125	100	43	93	138	112	96
To other federal agency	13,705	13,984	14,307	15,093	15,135	11,596	10,844	13,272	13,450
Resigned	50,321	47,976	48,903	44,692	38,859	39,334	40,579	47,408	47,687
Retired	49,091	48,275	44,625	42,150	42,125	50,886	54,373	60,035	58,904
Fired, other separations, reductions in force	13,350	13,301	12,623	12,450	13,328	15,828	14,524	15,933	14,929

Source: GAO analysis of CPDF data.

References

[1] GAO, 21st Century Challenges: Reexamining the Base of the Federal Government, GAO-05-325SP (Washington, D.C.: February 2005).

[2] See, e.g., section 1206 of the Financial Institutions Reform, Recovery, and Enforcement Act of 1989 (FIRREA), Pub. L. No. 101-73. See also, H. Conf. Rpt. No. 101-222, 457-458 (1989). While FIRREA uses "compensation" to mean "pay," for purposes of this report, compensation is defined as employee pay and benefits.

[3] GAO, Human Capital: Preliminary Observations on the Administration's Draft Proposed "Working for America Act," GAO-06-142T (Washington, D.C.: Oct. 5, 2005); Human Capital: Senior Executive Performance Management Can Be Significantly Strengthened to Achieve Results, GAO-04-614 (Washington, D.C.: May 26, 2004); and Results-Oriented Cultures, Creating a Clear Linkage between Individual and Organizational Success, GAO-03-488 (Washington, D.C.: Mar. 14, 2003).

[4] GAO, Human Capital: Implementing Pay for Performance at Selected Personnel Demonstration Projects, GAO-04-83 (Washington, D.C.: Jan. 23, 2004).

[5] The other three key practices are: provide and routinely use performance information to track organizational priorities, require follow-up actions to address organizational priorities, and maintain continuity during transitions.

[6] The smallest number of performance plans we examined from an agency was 1, in a case where the performance plans for all employees are completely standardized, and the largest number of plans we reviewed from an agency was 32. See table 3 in appendix I for more information on the dates of the performance appraisal cycles we reviewed at each agency.

[7] Resignations do not include employees who left an agency due to retirement.

[8] Pub. L. No. 101-73, section 1206, 103 Stat. 183, 523 (Aug. 9, 1989).

[9] Sections 301, 702, 1202-3, and 1210 of Pub. L. No. 101-73.

[10] Section 1315 of the Federal Housing Enterprises Financial Safety and Soundness Act of 1992, Pub. L. No. 102-550, 106 Stat. 3941 (1992).

[11] Section 8(a) of the Investor and Capital Markets Fee Relief Act, Pub. L. No. 107-123, 115 Stat. 2390 (2002).

[12] Section 10702(a) of the Farm Security and Rural Investment Act of 2002, Pub. L. No. 107-171, 116 Stat. 516 (2002).

[13] GAO-03-488.

[14] GAO-04-614.

[15] The other four practices are (1) align individual performance expectations with organizational goals, (2) connect performance expectations to crosscutting goals, (3) use competencies to provide a fuller assessment of performance, and (4) involve employees and stakeholders to gain ownership of performance management systems; the financial regulators have implemented these important practices in various ways.

[16] SEC had two distinct performance appraisal cycles, one for senior officers and one for all other employees. The completed cycles we examined were as follows: for senior officers from October 2004 to September 2005; for all other employees from May 2005 to April 2006.

[17] According to SEC officials, all employees received the annual across-the-board pay increase that all GS employees received.

[18] During the completed performance appraisal cycle we reviewed for CFTC (July 1, 2005, to June 30, 2006), the agency operated under a performance management system in which the only increases directly linked to performance ratings were some performance bonuses. In October 2006, CFTC introduced a new performance management system directive that affects the performance planning and appraisal processes. The agency will introduce an accompanying new pay policy in July 2007 that will complete the transition to a performance-based pay system under which merit increases will be linked to performance ratings. The new system was developed by an agency committee with employee and union input and the final approved system took effect on October 1, 2006. (The American Federation of Government Employees union has chapters at CFTC's Chicago and New York offices.) CFTC officials informed us that they do not plan to continue the annual pay adjustments in the new system, but will continue to use locality pay percentages equivalent to General Schedule executive order locality percentage increases.

[19] In the collective bargaining agreement for years 2006-2009, pay group 1 will receive a 5 percent pay increase and 1 percent lump sum payment, pay group 2 will receive a 3.2 percent pay increase and 1 percent lump sum, and pay group 3 will receive a 2.4 percent pay increase. Pay group 4, containing individuals who did not receive a "meets expectations" rating in the first appraisal process, will receive no increase.

[20] Section 4301 of Title 5 of the U.S. Code defines unacceptable performance as failure to meet established performance standards in one or more critical performance elements.

[21] SEC used "steps" to indicate performance-based pay increases. Zero steps meant no increase, one step corresponded to an increase of 1.47 percent, two steps to an increase of 2.94 percent, and three steps to an increase of 4.41 percent.

[22] GAO-06-142T and GAO-04-614.

[23] See appendix III for a discussion of different ways in which agencies budgeted for performance-based increases, including use of funding pools.

[24] GAO-03-488.

[25] GAO-06-142T.

[26] Rating levels at the agencies that accounted for less than 3 percent of employees included the following categories: "unacceptable," "unsatisfactory," "unsuccessful," "minimally acceptable," "minimally successful," "marginal," and "does not meet expectations."

[27] Securities and Exchange Commission, Office of the Inspector General, Enforcement Performance Management, Audit Report No. 423 (Feb. 8, 2007).

[28] See appendix I for our criteria for selecting mission-critical occupations in our study. We excluded executives from the analysis of average actual pay and pay scale. In addition, with the exception of the Federal Reserve Board and OFHEO, which do not have separate base and locality pay, the base pay shown in figure 3 does not include locality pay percentages.

[29] The analysis of employee movement does not include data for the Federal Reserve Board, because the CPDF does not include data for the agency.

[30] The "all other" category combines specialists in occupations such as human resources management, administration, clerical, management and program analysis, financial administration, and paralegal work. The three occupational categories with employee movement were attorney, examiner, and supervisor.

APPENDIX I

[1] The performance appraisal and pay systems at FDIC and SEC were sufficiently different from those of the other eight agencies that a correlation coefficient would not be a useful descriptor of the relationship between ratings and pay increases at these two agencies. Both FDIC and SEC use two-phase performance management systems that preclude the meaningful use of a single correlation coefficient. Neither the first or second processes in their systems are sufficiently comparable to the multilevel performance rating scales and pay increase determinations used at the other financial regulators. In the first process at FDIC and SEC, almost all employees were rated as "acceptable" on what was

essentially a two-level, "acceptable/unacceptable" rating scale. The lack of variation in performance ratings given in the first process would show little association with pay increases, and computing a correlation for this step would yield a coefficient at or around zero. In the second process, which was not considered to be a performance rating at these agencies, employees were assigned to performance groups at FDIC or awarded steps at SEC that were associated with specified percentage increases in pay. Computing a correlation between group assignment or steps awarded and percentage of pay increase would yield a perfect correlation since group or step assignment was synonymous with a specific percentage increase in pay.

[2] OPM's six occupational categories are Professional, Administrative, Technical, Clerical, Other White-Collar, and Blue Collar, collectively known as "PATCOB." When we sent the list of mission critical occupations to the agencies, we listed the occupational title and asked the agency to identify the OPM job series number they used for that occupation. For some occupations, all agencies used the same job series (for example, 0905 for attorneys). For other occupations, some agencies used different job series for the same or similar occupation (for example, agencies used several agency-unique job series for "examiners" such as 1831, 0580, and 0570). Two agencies (CFTC and OFHEO) placed employees in the same job series (1801 for CFTC and 0501 for OFHEO) into two different occupations (examiners and investigators, and examiners and financial analysts, respectively). In both cases, we placed all employees in the examiner occupation because the CPDF does not facilitate separating employees with the same job series into separate occupations. For a few occupations, some agencies used an OPM job series number that we did not expect (for example, OFHEO used 0301 for information technology specialists and FCA used 1101 for examiners). When we analyzed CPDF data, we used the occupational titles and job series numbers the agencies provided to us. Executives were not included in the pay analyses. We excluded executives from the analysis of average actual pay and pay scale, because we wanted to focus on mid-level management.

[3] We were not able to always find a transfer-in personnel action to match a transfer-out personnel action within the time frames stipulated for transfers. Some transfer-in personnel actions that we did not find in fiscal year 1990 could be due to the fact that the transfer-out personnel action occurred in fiscal year 1989. Similarly, some of the transfer-out personnel actions in fiscal year 2006 for which we did not find a matching transfer-in personnel action could be due to the fact that they occurred in fiscal year 2007.

APPENDIX III

[1] According to OPM, performance elements identify the activities, skills, or responsibilities that the employee is expected to achieve during the year and performance standards identify how well the employee must meet each performance element to receive a specific performance rating.

[2] Federal Deposit Insurance Corporation, Performance Management Program, Directive System Circular 2430.1, Mar. 28, 2002.

[3] GAO-04-614; GAO, Managing for Results: Emerging Benefits From Selected Agencies' Use of Performance Agreements, GAO-01-115, Washington, D.C.: (Oct. 30, 2000).

[4] GAO, Human Capital: Managing Human Capital in the 21st Century, GAO/T-GGD-00-77 (Washington, D.C.: Mar. 9, 2000).

[5] GAO-04-614.

[6] Basel II is a set of proposed changes to the original set of risk-based capital rules based on an internationally adopted framework developed by the Basel Committee. In the United States, Basel II rules are intended to apply primarily to the largest and most internationally active banking organizations.

[7] GAO-04-614.

[8] According to an agency official, OFHEO's weighting system is expected to be modified as revisions are made to the performance management system.

[9] Employees at FDIC, NCUA, OCC, and SEC are represented by the National Treasury Employees Union. OTS employees in Washington, D.C., and CFTC staff at two offices are represented by the American Federation of Government Employees.

[10] GAO, Human Capital: Practices that Empowered and Involved Employees, GAO-01-1070 (Washington, D.C.: Sept. 14, 2001).

[11] The Federal Service Impasses Panel is part of the Federal Labor Relations Authority and resolves impasses between federal agencies and labor unions representing federal employees arising from negotiations over conditions of employment. The Panel may make recommendations to the parties on how to overcome the impasse, if bargaining and mediation are unsuccessful.

[12] We did not assess whether meetings involving employees in performance planning or appraisals were conducted in accordance with agency policy or the quality of the interactions between supervisors and employees. We relied on representatives from employee groups and unions to describe their perceptions of actual employee participation in expectation-setting meetings and their perceptions of management's consideration of employee input into appraisals.

[13] According to OCC officials, generic performance plans are established for examiners because they all perform similar functions. The primary objectives in these standardized plans are generic. Any additional primary objectives or

secondary objectives included in the examiner performance plans are tailored to individuals. According to officials, commissioned examiners should have at least one secondary objective in their performance plans so that they have the potential to receive a level 4 (highest) performance rating. Precommissioned examiners, who are focused on completing a rigorous training program, are not required to have secondary performance objectives, although they are not prohibited from having them.

[14] A correlation coefficient is a measure of association (strength) of the relationship between two variables; in this case, ratings and percentage increases in pay. A positive correlation coefficient would mean that the two variables tend to increase (or decrease) together. A positive coefficient would indicate that as the rating goes up, so does the percentage increase in pay. A negative coefficient would mean that the two factors have an inverse relationship—as one variable increases, the other decreases. Values of the coefficient may range from -1.0 to +1.0. The percentage increase in ratings-linked pay was based on the combined value of both increases in base pay and lump sum (one time) payments, relative to prior annual salary. The performance appraisal and performance-based pay systems at FDIC and SEC were sufficiently different from the other eight agencies that we do not include correlation coefficients for these two agencies. See appendix I, Objectives, Scope, and Methodology, for additional information concerning the exclusion of FDIC and SEC from this analysis.

[15] In those instances where agency rating scales used lower numeric values to indicate higher performance levels, the values were reversed so that all coefficients would reflect the relationship of an increase in ratings with an increase in pay as a positive coefficient.

[16] See appendix I for additional information on the limitations of the correlation coefficient.

[17] Officials at one agency told us that setting separate budget amounts for merit pay increases for each unit helped to ensure that merit pay resources were more fairly distributed across the units.

[18] GAO-06-142T.

APPENDIX IV

[1] For the six FIRREA financial regulatory agencies (FCA, FDIC, FHFB, NCUA, OCC, and OTS), see sections 301, 702, 120-3, 1206, and 1210 of the Financial Institutions Reform, Recovery, and Enforcement Act of 1989, Pub. L. No. 101-73 (1989); for OFHEO, section 1315 of Pub. L. No. 102-550 (1992); for SEC, section 8(a) of Pub. L. No. 107-123 (2002), and for CFTC, section 10702 (a) of Pub. L. No. 107-171 (2002).

[2] While many of the financial regulatory agencies received increased flexibility under FIRREA in 1989, such flexibility was afforded to OFHEO in 1992 and to CFTC and SEC in 2002.

[3] GAO, Results-Oriented Government: Practices That Can Help Enhance and Sustain Collaboration among Federal Agencies, GAO-06-15 (Washington, D.C.: Oct. 21, 2005).

[4] We did not include the Federal Reserve Board and OFHEO in our example on differences in agencies' base pay because the Federal Reserve Board and OFHEO's base pay include the element equivalent to other agencies' locality pay for Washington, D.C.

[5] In addition to these five agencies, FCA offered a 401(k) plan but discontinued it in December 2006.

APPENDIX V

[1] The data in these tables are for permanent employees only.

INDEX

D

E

I

J

L

M

N

S

T

U

V

W

Y